Merry Christmas!
2017

BEACH
Cocktails

COASTAL
LIVING

BEACH
Cocktails

**Favorite SURFSIDE
SIPS and BAR SNACKS**

Oxmoor
House®

Published by Oxmoor House, an imprint of Time Inc. Books
225 Liberty Street, New York, NY 10281

Senior Editor: Katherine Cobbs
Project Editor: Melissa Brown
Designer: Amy Bickell
Junior Designer: Olivia Pierce
Photographers: Iain Bagwell, Robbie Caponetto, Jennifer Causey, Jennifer Davick, Tara Donne,
   Greg Dupree, David Hanson, David Hillegas, Becky Luigart-Stayner, Alison Miksch,
   Con Poulos, Victor Protasio, Jessica Sample, Brian Woodcock, Dasha Wright
Prop Stylists: Jessie Baude, Mary Clayton Carl, Kay E. Clarke, Audrey Davis,
   Morgan Locke, Lindsey Lower, Amy Stone
Food Stylists: Torie Cox, Margaret Monroe Dickey, Rishon Hanners, Tami Hardeman,
   Katelyn Hardwick
Recipe Developers and Testers: Katherine Cobbs, Mark Driskill, Paige Grandjean,
   Emily Nabors Hall, Julia Levy, Pam Lolley, Karen Rankin
Senior Production Manager: Greg A. Amason
Assistant Production and Project Manager: Lauren Moriarty
Copy Editors: Adrienne Davis, Ashley Strickland Freeman
Proofreaders: Donna Baldone, Jacqueline Giovanelli
Indexer: Carol Roberts
Fellows: Helena Joseph, Hailey Middlebrook, Kyle Grace Mills

Photography Credits:
   Tony Novak-Clifford: 62-63; **Julien Capmeil:** 124; **Courtesy of Sea Island:** 161
   Getty Images: Jonathan Bird: 23; David Sacks: 26; surachetkhamsuk: 30-31; karandaev: 45;
   Colin Anderson: 47; For the love of photography: 48; Jane Sweeney: 72; Bryan Mullennix: 77;
   atosan: 82; Alexcrab: 111; Emad Aljumah: 114; Richard Felber: 116; Pam Ullman: 122; Fraser Hall:
   128; ©fitopardo.com: 142; elisalocci: 150-151; tuneman1980: 155; Michael Utech: 159; Nancy
   Nehring: 163; Dave G Kelly: 166; mikolajn: 180; Stephen Saks: 186; Macduff Everton: 188-189;
   Courtney Keating: 196-197; FRILET Patrick / hemis.fr: 203; apomares: 211; CathyRL: 213;
   Silvrshootr: 218; MikeMareen: 220; Arturo Pe?a Romano Medina: 231; JuiceEllis: 235; JackF:
   238-239; Punchalit Chotikasatian: 240; asya_mix: 252-253; travelstock44 / LOOK-foto:
   268; traveler1116: 272; Nottomanv1: 14-15, 24-35, 88-89, 138-139, 172-173, 194-195, 228-229;
   jpgfactory: endsheets; **Shutterstock:** stockcreations: drink on cover

ISBN-13: 978-0-8487-5219-4
Library of Congress Control Number: 2016955718

First Edition 2017
Printed in China
10 9 8 7 6 5 4 3 2

We welcome your comments and suggestions about Time Inc. Books. Please write to us at:
Time Inc. Books
Attention: Book Editors
P.O. Box 62310
Tampa, Florida 33662-2310

Time Inc. Books products may be purchased for business or promotional use. For
information on bulk purchases, please contact Christi Crowley in the Special Sales
Department at (845) 895-9858.

Contents

Why drinks taste better at the beach

BY JONATHAN MILES

I'VE OFTEN WONDERED why cocktails offered within sight or sound of the ocean taste better than those served inland. The theory I've developed, with glass in hand, goes like this: A sip of whiskey in a snowbound mountain cabin tastes grand, as does an after-work martini in an urban saloon. But what these drinks do so well, I think, is to readjust one's balance in the face of unruly circumstances—the frigid air outside that cabin, the honking traffic outside that bar. Their effect is often medicinal—they relieve the symptoms of life. For many, however, the ocean provides that same analgesic effect. A cocktail served by the shore, then, doesn't so much repair as enhance. It gilds the lily of life.

But maybe there are other factors at work, too. Consider, for instance, one of my favorite summertime refreshments. It's a simple mixture of gin and coconut water made rust-colored and faintly savory by the addition of angostura bitters. At my home, an hour from the shore, it's a fine drink—tasty, invigorating, evocative. Yet when consumed in its natural habitat, as when I recently drank one or two in the Bahamas, it's genuinely mind-blowing. What my tongue was tasting felt aligned with what my eyes were seeing: a postcard vista of sea, sand, and rosy sky. I'm reminded of an itty-bitty beach bar in the Galápagos Islands I once stumbled upon, a grove of hammocks surrounding an alfresco bar above which hung a sign reading, "Endemic Cocktails." When I asked what the sign meant, the owner waved at the hammocks and the big blue Pacific beyond and said, "It means I serve drinks that make sense to drink here."

That alignment might also explain why a margarita—that ubiquitous staple of mall restaurants everywhere—tastes so keenly superior when sipped by a beach. Cocktail historians can't say for certain where the margarita originated, but the leading candidates are all beach towns: Ensenada, Tijuana, Galveston, Acapulco. That makes sense to me because the combination of briny blanco tequila and lime seems oceanically inspired. The recipe I swear by is derived from San Francisco bartender Julio Bermejo, and came to me via Joanne Weir's book *Tequila*. This adaptation is a bracingly minimalist take, a bikini of a recipe: just tequila, lime, and agave nectar, plus water and salt. I haven't deviated from this recipe in six years and cannot imagine a reason to ever do so.

The relationship between rum and the sea is as cultural as it is gustatory. The original use for rum was as a substitute for water and beer—both tended to spoil—on long sea voyages, which is why we associate it with sailors, pirates, and yo ho ho. Lime and sugar have been chaperones for the rum-sea pairing almost from the beginning, but when Bermudans added ginger to the formula, about a century ago, they invented a dockside classic. That's the Dark 'n' Stormy, a merger of Gosling's Black Seal rum and ginger beer that tastes like far more than the sum of its parts. It's a straightforward highball that carries itself like a maritime potion. And like the margarita, and like the tropical sublimity of the gin-coconut water combination, it's a drink that tastes not just grand, but perfectly grand, when blessed by proximity to the sea that inspired it.

Jonathan Miles is the author of the novels Dear American Airlines *and* Want Not. *He lives on the banks of the Delaware River in western New Jersey.*

Bar Tools

Get the goods for masterful cocktail mixing or just to look like a pro.

BAR SPOON: A long-handled spoon for stirring, muddling, and measuring.

COCKTAIL SHAKERS: For vigorous mixing, a Boston Shaker is a small glass that locks inside a large steel cup; a Cobbler Shaker swaps a mixing glass for a metal cap.

BOTTLE OPENER: Pops off caps; pick one with a pointed can punch.

CITRUS SQUEEZER: A handy metal press that snugly fits lemons and limes, allowing for easy juice extraction.

FINE STRAINER: Blocks fruit pulp and herbs from entering the drink.

HAWTHORNE STRAINER: An all-purpose strainer with a tight coil that fits tightly on a shaker, ensuring no spillage.

ICE PICK: Strong, sturdy, metal spike for breaking up blocks of ice.

JIGGER: Stainless steel, conical, and akin to a two-sided shot glass, this tool provides precise measurements for cocktail mixing.

JULEP STRAINER: A round, metal disk with holes that fits tightly to a cocktail rim. Ideal for straining cocktails from a mixing glass.

MICROPLANE: A slender grater that is perfect for shaving orange or lemon zests, as well as woody spices like cinnamon sticks or nutmeg.

MUDDLER: Used for crushing herbs, sugar cubes, and fruit in cocktails.

SWIZZLE: A spoked tool originally made from a woody stem now fashioned from plastic or glass used to mix icy drinks.

WAITER'S CORKSCREW: Better than a standard, bulky corkscrew, this option folds like a pocket knife and has an attached bottle opener.

Y PEELER: A versatile metal peeler that can handle both small and large citrus fruits.

Glassware

The right glass for a drink is like the right shoes for an outfit.

COLLINS: 14 ounces; The tall, slim, column-shaped glass is perfect for serving the eponymous Tom Collins and other fizzy drinks.

COUPE: 4 to 6 ounces; The stemmed, shallow, widemouthed glass designed for Champagne is better for cocktails served straight up.

FLUTE: 6 to 9 ounces; The stemmed, narrow body of a flute is ideal for Champagne's bubbles, but other effervescent cocktails shine, too.

HEATPROOF GLASS OR MUG: 12 to 16 ounces; Handled, heatproof glassware is ideal for warm drinks like hot toddies or Irish coffee.

HIGHBALL: 8 to 12 ounces; Tall and straight like the Collins glass, only shorter, highballs are best for fizzy cocktails like gin and tonics.

HURRICANE: 20 ounces; The tall, short-stemmed glass that flairs at the lip is used for a variety of mixed drinks, particularly its namesake.

JULEP CUP: 8 to 10 ounces; Short, and usually silver or copper, classic metal-plated julep cups keep minty juleps and Moscow Mules frosty.

MARGARITA: 12 ounces; A stemmed, generous widemouthed glass with a wide rim perfect for twisting in salt.

MARTINI: 4 to 6 ounces; The stemmed glass with a conical cup is the classic vessel whether you like your martini shaken or stirred.

PILSNER: 10 to 16 ounces; The tall, V-shaped glass holds tap beers or ales, as well as large drinks with extravagant garnishes.

ROCKS (or Old-Fashioned): 6 to 8 ounces for single, 12 to 14 ounces for double; The short glass is for drinks served neat (no ice) or on the rocks.

TIKI MUG: Sizes vary; Whimsical, Polynesian-themed tiki mugs come in many forms, from giant wooden pineapples to totem motifs.

WINEGLASS: 8 to 12 ounces; Red wineglasses are shorter and have a rounder bowl with a wider mouth than white wineglasses.

The Art of the Garnish

Edible or nonedible, garnishes are the crowning jewels of the cocktail glass that can be used in inspired ways to elevate any beverage, spirited or not.

Garnishes add visual interest, but also impart flavor and fragrance. Whether you top your toddy with a tiki umbrella or stir your Bloody Mary with a loaded skewer of pickled goodness, the garnish is an opportunity to dress up a drink in eye-catching style. Get creative and think beyond the wedge and twist.

Frozen berries, fruit cubes, or melon balls chill cocktails without diluting them. Citrus fruits, in particular, add sunny color and a tropical flourish to the glass. Lemon, lime, orange, and grapefruit juices impart bright flavor notes while the citrus oils from a rind twisted over a glass lend not only flavor but the aromatic essence of the fruit, which primes the palate even before the first sip.

Float pretty ice cubes, which can be made by freezing juices or fresh fruit with water in ice cube trays. Make a natural skewer from a sliver of peeled sugarcane, a thin stalk of lemongrass, or a pineapple leaf for an unexpected, ornamental surprise.

Pickled and brined ingredients like okra, caper berries, cocktail onions, and olives add a savory note to cocktails. Look to your salty, vinegary, preserved pantry staples for inspiration.

The enjoyment of a cocktail is one of life's simple pleasures and an experience to savor. Any way you slice, dice, or skewer it, always consider the final accessory for a perfectly composed cocktail.

IN THE MIX

simple syrup

Blend sweetness into cold drinks with this sublimely versatile syrup.

MAKES 1¼ CUPS

Combine the water and sugar in a saucepan over medium-high heat. Boil until the sugar dissolves. Remove from heat, and let stand 30 minutes. Strain and chill until ready to use.

VARIATION:

mint simple syrup: Add 1½ cups fresh mint leaves to the water and sugar mixture and proceed with the recipe.

1	CUP WATER
1	CUP (8 OUNCES) SUGAR

lime-basil simple syrup

This syrup adds exotic flavor to our Basil Tonic (page 113).

MAKES ABOUT ⅔ CUP

Combine the water and sugar in a small saucepan. Cook over medium-high heat until the sugar dissolves, about 12 minutes. Remove from heat, and stir in fresh lime zest and basil sprig. Steep 10 minutes and then cool for 1 hour. Strain and chill.

½	CUP WATER
½	CUP (4 OUNCES) SUGAR
1	TABLESPOON LIME ZEST
1	LARGE FRESH BASIL SPRIG

lemongrass simple syrup

This adds a bright citrusy zing to Pineapple Mojitos (page 206).

MAKES 1¼ CUPS

1 Combine the sugar, water, and salt in a small saucepan over medium-high heat. Bring to a boil, stirring occasionally, until sugar dissolves. Remove from heat.

2 Trim both ends of the lemongrass stalks, and remove coarse outside leaves. Cut into 3-inch pieces, and crush to break up fibers. Place lemongrass in sugar mixture, and let stand 30 minutes. Transfer to a glass container; cover and chill overnight. Strain syrup, discarding lemongrass, and chill.

1	CUP (8 OUNCES) SUGAR
1	CUP WATER
	PINCH OF SALT
2	(12-INCH) FRESH LEMONGRASS STALKS

jalapeño-honey syrup

1 JALAPEÑO CHILE, HALVED
½ CUP HONEY
½ CUP BOILING WATER

Seed the jalapeño for less spiciness in this uncommon syrup that lends sweet heat to cocktails like our Christopher Robin (page 113).

MAKES ¾ CUP

Stir together all the ingredients; steep 1 hour. Strain.

ginger-honey syrup

¼ CUP CHOPPED FRESH GINGER
1 TABLESPOON FINELY MINCED LIME ZEST
1 CUP WATER
1½ CUPS HONEY

This syrup adds a spicy shot to Zesty Ginger-Lime Cooler (page 91). Keep the syrup in the refrigerator up to two weeks so you'll be ready to mix up this favorite cocktail anytime.

MAKES 2 CUPS

Combine all the ingredients in a small saucepan. Bring to a boil over medium-high heat; reduce heat, and simmer 2 minutes. Remove from heat; let stand 1 hour. Strain mixture through a fine wire-mesh strainer, discarding solids. Store in refrigerator up to 2 weeks.

strawberry syrup

Pressing jam through a sieve is a shortcut to a flavorful fruit syrup. Try orange marmalade thinned with orange flower water or cherry jam thinned with Kirsch, a cherry brandy.

MAKES ABOUT ⅓ CUP

Combine the strawberry jam and grenadine in a small bowl. Press through a fine wire-mesh strainer, discarding solids.

¼ CUP STRAWBERRY JAM

1½ TABLESPOONS GRENADINE (PAGE 23)

cucumber simple syrup

This fresh syrup is perfect in a Pimm's Cup (page 133), an ice-cold glass of lemonade, or tequila over ice with a squeeze of lime.

MAKES 1¼ CUPS

Bring the water and sugar to a boil in a small saucepan over medium-high heat, stirring constantly until sugar dissolves. Cool. Combine cooled syrup and cucumber in a food processor; process until well blended. Steep 1 hour; strain. Store in an airtight container in the refrigerator up to 5 days.

1 CUP WATER

1 CUP (8 OUNCES) SUGAR

1 ENGLISH CUCUMBER, PEELED AND COARSELY CHOPPED

toasted orgeat syrup

Nutty orgeat (OR-JAY), from the French "orge" for barley, is a sweet syrup originally made with barley and almonds. Try it in our Grapefruit Trinidad Sour (page 136).

MAKES 1 CUP

1½ CUPS DEMERARA SUGAR

1¼ CUPS WATER

10 OUNCES (ABOUT 2 CUPS) RAW SKIN-ON ALMONDS, LIGHTLY CHOPPED AND TOASTED

1 OUNCE (2 TABLESPOONS) VODKA

1 TEASPOON ORANGE BLOSSOM WATER

Combine the sugar and water in a saucepan over medium-high. Boil, stirring, until sugar melts. Cook, stirring, 1 minute. Add nuts; cook, stirring, 1 minute. Remove from heat; let stand 3 hours. Pour through a wire-mesh strainer into a bowl; discard solids. Transfer to a glass jar with a lid. Stir in the vodka and orange blossom water. Cover and store in refrigerator up to 2 weeks.

falernum syrup

Aromatics and spices come together in this classic tiki syrup.

MAKES ABOUT 5½ CUPS

1 (10-OUNCE) PACKAGE BLANCHED WHOLE ALMONDS, CHOPPED

2 QUARTS DISTILLED WATER

1 TABLESPOON CARDAMOM PODS

1 TABLESPOON CORIANDER SEEDS

2 TEASPOONS WHOLE CLOVES

3 STAR ANISE PODS

4 CUPS CANE SUGAR

½ CUP CHOPPED PEELED FRESH GINGER (4-INCH PIECE)

3 LARGE LEMON PEEL STRIPS, CHOPPED

7 OUNCES (¾ CUP PLUS 2 TABLESPOONS) OVENPROOF RUM (SUCH AS BACARDI 151)

1 Place the nuts in a large jar with a lid. Add 1 quart of the distilled water; seal and let stand 30 minutes, shaking every 10 minutes. Drain the almonds. Rinse jar, and return nuts to jar. Add remaining distilled water. Cover and chill 4 hours, shaking occasionally.

2 Combine the whole spices in a large saucepan over medium-high, stirring often, until fragrant, about 1 minute. Stir in the sugar, ginger, and chilled nuts (including water). Clean and dry jar; set aside. Boil mixture, stirring often; remove from heat. Stir in chopped lemon peel; let stand until cool, about 1 hour.

3 Return the mixture to clean jar. Cover and chill 8 hours.

4 Pour the mixture through a fine wire-mesh strainer lined with 2 layers of cheesecloth, pressing on solids to extract liquid. Discard solids. Stir in the rum. Divide the mixture among clean glass jars; cover with lids, and store in refrigerator up to 2 weeks.

GRENADINES

Surprisingly, pomegranates aren't grown on this 32-island chain that shares the cocktail syrup's name.

grenadine

Derived from the French "grenade" and Spanish "grenada," which both refer to the pomegranate, today's store-bought grenadine is made mostly of corn syrup, artificial flavors, and food dye. This homemade syrup is flavorful and simple to make but not as atomic red a mixer as its commercial cousin.

MAKES 1 PINT

Combine the sugar and juice in a quart-size glass jar with a tight-fitting lid. Cover jar with lid, and swirl until sugar is dissolved, 2 to 3 minutes. Add pomegranate molasses, vodka, and orange blossom water. Cover with lid, and shake gently to combine. Store in refrigerator up to 2 weeks.

- 1 CUP SUPERFINE SUGAR
- 1 CUP POMEGRANATE-CHERRY JUICE, AT ROOM TEMPERATURE
- ¼ CUP BOTTLED POMEGRANATE MOLASSES
- 1 OUNCE (2 TABLESPOONS) VODKA
- 2 TEASPOONS ORANGE BLOSSOM WATER

sweet-and-sour mix

- 1 CUP (8 OUNCES) SUGAR
- 1 CUP WATER
- 1 CUP (8 OUNCES) FRESH LEMON JUICE
- 1 CUP (8 OUNCES) FRESH LIME JUICE

Sweeten your favorite tiki cocktail with this tart-sweet mixer that also makes an appearance in the Summer Sangria (page 227).

MAKES 2¼ CUPS

Combine the sugar and water in a saucepan over medium heat. Cook, stirring often, until sugar dissolves. Remove from heat. Stir in the lemon and lime juices. Cover and chill.

sour mix

- 1 CUP (8 OUNCES) SUGAR
- 2 LARGE PASTEURIZED EGG WHITES
- ½ CUP (4 OUNCES) FRESH LIME JUICE
- ¼ CUP (2 OUNCES) FRESH LEMON JUICE
- ¼ CUP (2 OUNCES) FRESH ORANGE JUICE
- 2 CUPS WATER

More tart than sweet, this sour mix lends more than flavor to drinks. The addition of egg whites adds body to the mix, giving cocktails a rich mouthfeel. Our Palm Beach Martini (page 117) is a perfect example to sample.

MAKES ABOUT 3 CUPS

Stir together all the ingredients until sugar dissolves and mixture is well blended.

Bitter Cure

DEEP IN THE HEART OF VENEZUELA IN THE 1820s, in a port town called Angostura, now Ciudad Bolívar, a German doctor named Johann Seigert had a puzzling task: finding a cure for seasickness and tropical diseases like malaria. Each day, Seigert would tend to a new wave of weary Venezuelan soldiers, many who complained of stomach aches and fevers made worse by the tropical climate. The doctor was convinced he could find a natural cure, using plants that grew along the fertile Orinoco River. After mixing alcohol with different herbs, spices, and botanicals, he eventually found the perfect combination: He called his concoction Angostura Aromatic Bitters.

Seigert's remedy was instantly popular among sailors. Bitters allegedly had the power to settle upset stomachs, relieve fevers, and even cure hiccups. It was so popular that Seigert opened a distillery in Angostura to produce bitters in 1830, though he kept his recipe top-secret. Talk of the miracle restorative from Angostura soon traveled to Port of Spain, Trinidad, where Seigert would eventually relocate his business.

To this day, the exact recipe for Angostura Bitters—and thus its seasickness-curing properties—remains a mystery, though bitters are a staple in classic cocktails such as the Manhattan, Old Fashioned, and the Pisco Sour.

homemade peach-vanilla bitters

Bitters are infinitely adaptable by substituting different flavored syrups for the one used here. Due to a high alcohol content, it keeps indefinitely in a cool, dark place. Wormwood is a woody herb that can be found at spice stores, such as Penzeys.

MAKES ⅔ CUP

1 Day 1, prepare Aromatic Mixture: Combine first 6 ingredients in a small glass jar. Cover and let stand in a cool, dark place 10 days.

2 Day 11, pour mixture through a wire-mesh strainer into a bowl; reserve vodka. Place solids in a saucepan. Add the water. Boil over high and remove from heat; let stand 5 minutes. Pour (with solids) into vodka. Cover. Let stand in a cool, dark place 5 days.

3 Prepare Bitters Mixture: Combine first 4 ingredients in a clean jar. Cover and let stand in a cool, dark place 2 days.

4 Day 13, pour Bitters Mixture through a wire-mesh strainer into a bowl; reserve vodka. Place solids in a saucepan. Add water. Boil over high and remove from heat; let stand 5 minutes. Pour (with solids) into vodka. Cover. Let stand 2 days. Pour through strainer into a jar; discard solids. Cover. Store in a cool, dark place.

5 Day 15, pour Aromatic Mixture through a wire-mesh strainer into a jar; discard solids. Cover. Store in a cool, dark place.

6 Prepare Peach-Vanilla Syrup: Combine all ingredients in a medium saucepan over medium-high. Boil, stirring often, until sugar dissolves. Remove from heat; let stand, uncovered, 1 hour.

7 Pour peach mixture through a wire-mesh strainer into a bowl, pressing lightly on solids to extract juices. Scrape inside of vanilla bean with the back of a paring knife; add vanilla seeds to peach syrup. Discard vanilla bean and solids.

8 Prepare Peach-Vanilla Bitters: Combine ¼ cup Aromatic Mixture, ⅛ cup Bitters Mixture, and ⅜ cup Peach-Vanilla Syrup. Reserve remaining Peach-Vanilla Syrup for cocktails and remaining Aromatic Mixture and Bitters Mixture for making other bitters flavors. Store in a clean, lidded jar at room temperature.

AROMATIC MIXTURE:

4   OUNCES (½ CUP) VODKA

2   OUNCES (¼ CUP) PURE GRAIN ALCOHOL

2   TABLESPOONS DRIED LEMON PEEL

2   TABLESPOONS GROUND CORIANDER

2   TABLESPOONS GROUND FENNEL

1   TABLESPOON DRIED ORANGE PEEL

½   CUP PLUS 2 TABLESPOONS WATER

BITTERS MIXTURE:

6   OUNCES (¾ CUP) VODKA

2   OUNCES (¼ CUP) PURE GRAIN ALCOHOL

2   TABLESPOONS DRIED GENTIAN ROOT

1   TABLESPOON DRIED WORMWOOD

½   CUP PLUS 2 TABLESPOONS WATER

PEACH-VANILLA SYRUP:

1   CUP CHOPPED DRIED PEACHES

1   CUP (8 OUNCES) SUGAR

1   CUP WATER

1   VANILLA BEAN, CUT IN HALF LENGTHWISE

1   FRESH LEMONGRASS STALK, CUT INTO THIRDS AND CRUSHED LIGHTLY WITH THE BACK OF A KNIFE

lemongrass-citrus shrub syrup

Rich, bright citrus notes are well balanced with sweet and tangy elements from the cane sugar and champagne vinegar. Try a splash in your glass of seltzer for refreshment that beats any soda pop.

MAKES 1 QUART

2   CUPS CANE SUGAR

2   CUPS CHAMPAGNE VINEGAR

4   LEMONS, VERY THINLY SLICED (ABOUT 2 CUPS)

4   FRESH LEMONGRASS STALKS, TRIMMED, SMASHED, AND COARSELY CHOPPED (ABOUT 1½ CUPS)

1 Stir all ingredients in a glass bowl until sugar is dissolved, 1 minute. Cover. Let stand at room temperature 8 hours.

2 Pour through a wire-mesh strainer into a bowl. Squeeze solids with clean hands to extract all liquid. Discard solids. Pour into a jar with a tight-fitting lid. Cover and refrigerate up to 2 weeks.

pineapple shrub syrup

Spike straight rum or tequila on the rocks with a splash of this shrub, or drizzle over grilled pineapple, poundcake, or ice cream!

MAKES 1 PINT

1   CUP CANE SUGAR

½   CUP WATER

4   CUPS CHOPPED FRESH PINEAPPLE (FROM 1 PINEAPPLE)

¼   CUP UNSEASONED RICE VINEGAR

1 Combine sugar and water in a large saucepan over medium-high. Boil, stirring often. Stir in pineapple. Reduce to medium-low, and simmer, stirring, until fruit is very soft and begins to break down, 10 minutes. Remove from heat; mash fruit with a potato masher. Pour into a large glass bowl and cool completely. Cover and let stand at room temperature 8 hours.

2 Pour through a wire-mesh strainer into a bowl; discard solids. Place liquid in a jar. Stir in up to ¼ cup vinegar, 1 tablespoon at a time, to desired tanginess. Cover and refrigerate up to 2 weeks.

A Short History of Shrubs

THOUGHT TO HAVE ORIGINATED in England in the early 15th century, early shrubs were made with rum and fruit juice. They gained popularity, thanks to smugglers, in the 1680s. At the time, England had placed a high tariff on imported luxury goods, including rum and brandy. To avoid the steep price of shipment, and to keep their fellow Englishmen jolly, smugglers would sink barrels of alcohol off the shore of England and wait until the coast was clear. Upon a watchman's cue, the smugglers would retrieve the barrels from the sea and bring them to shore to be sold to merchants.

Unfortunately, the wooden barrels were not impenetrable to seawater. Rum and brandy bought from smugglers often had a slightly briny taste if it hadn't turned altogether. Worried that business might fail if customers weren't satisfied, smugglers searched for ways to mask the tainted flavor of the alcohol. Shrubs were the perfect solution: Sweet fruit juice masked the salty undertones. Shrubs also aged well. Unlike punch, a fruit-alcohol mixture that should be served immediately, shrubs can last several weeks without refrigeration, though we suggest keeping them chilled for best flavor.

Today's craft cocktail movement has brought about a shrub renaissance with a primary focus on "drinking vinegars" or shrubs that rely on vinegar instead of spirits. These tart syrups may be sipped over ice on their own or mixed into cocktails to add interest and build layered tart-sweet-fragrant flavor.

Salt is harvested by hand in Thailand, and then organized into neat rows that are cut into pyramids.

citrus rim salt (TOP LEFT)

This tangy salt garnish is tailor-made for margaritas and much more.

MAKES ABOUT ½ CUP

¼ CUP KOSHER SALT

¼ CUP GROUND CORIANDER

1 TEASPOON LEMON ZEST

1 TEASPOON LIME ZEST

1 TEASPOON GRAPEFRUIT ZEST

1 Pulse all ingredients in a food processor until thoroughly combined. Store in an airtight container at room temperature up to 2 weeks.

2 Sprinkle salt mixture onto a small plate. Dampen rim of glass with water or citrus juice. Twist rim in salt mixture to evenly coat.

bacon–bloody mary rim salt (MIDDLE)

Salt meets smoke in this mix that's perfect for bourbon cocktails, too.

MAKES ¾ CUP

6 COOKED BACON SLICES, CRUMBLED (ABOUT ⅓ CUP)

2 TABLESPOONS KOSHER SALT

2 TEASPOONS CELERY SEEDS

2 TEASPOONS PAPRIKA

½ TEASPOON SMOKED PAPRIKA

¼ CUP OLD BAY SEASONING

1 Pulse first 5 ingredients in a food processor until ground, 4 to 5 times. Transfer to a bowl; stir in Old Bay. (Mixture will be sticky.) Store in an airtight container at room temperature up to 1 week.

2 Sprinkle salt mixture on a plate. Dampen rim of glass with citrus juice or hot sauce. Twist rim in salt mixture to evenly coat.

sweet-and-sour rim salt (BOTTOM LEFT)

Pair this delicious salt with citrus-based cocktail spirits like gin.

MAKES ¾ CUP

½ CUP SUPERFINE SUGAR

¼ CUP FINE PINK SEA SALT

1½ TEASPOONS LEMON ZEST

1 Process all ingredients in a food processor until finely ground, 20 seconds. Store in an airtight container at room temperature up to 1 week.

2 Sprinkle salt mixture on a plate. Dampen rim of glass in citrus juice. Twist rim in salt mixture to evenly coat.

Tiki Bar Tales

Most people live on a lonely island, lost in the middle of a foggy sea. Most people long for another island, one where they know they will like to be.

SO BEGINS "BALI HA'I," from the 40s musical *South Pacific*—a tune that captures midcentury America's obsession with paradise. This song is sung by Bloody Mary, the matriarch of the fictitious island of Bali Ha'i, to young Lieutenant Cable, whom Mary hopes to lure to the island to fall for her daughter, Liat. But Bali Ha'i is an impossible fantasy, looming large, always just out of reach: A place where palm trees sway, waves lap the shore, ukuleles twang, and vivacious women pluck fruit from the vine. It is a paradise far from the darkness of war and dullness of corporate America.

The film fanned the flames of the tiki craze in America. At the helm of the trend was Ernest Gantt, aka Donn Beach, a former Texas bootlegger whose youth was spent island hopping. Stateside, Gantt was a Hollywood set designer, loaning his island souvenirs to film sets before opening his Polynesian-themed bar, Don's Beachcomber Café. He later expanded into what became the famous Don the Beachcomber restaurant.

The Beachcomber provided an escape. Exotic menu items enticed. Martinis were traded for rum cocktails in tiki mugs made with tropical syrups, and garnished with paper umbrellas. Gantt is credited for the Zombie, Navy Grog, and Mai Tai, which showcase his knack for masking potent cocktails with sweet island flavors.

Celebrities flocked to the restaurant, further adding to its allure. An evening there—and later, at Trader Vic's, a tiki bar that opened in Seattle in 1940—provided an escape from the everyday. At closing time, guests were allowed to keep their tiki mugs, like souvenirs from a trip to a farflung locale.

tequila sunrise

(COCKTAIL ON RIGHT)

⅓ CUP (ABOUT 2½ OUNCES) FRESH ORANGE JUICE (ABOUT 1 ORANGE)

3 TABLESPOONS (1½ OUNCES) SILVER TEQUILA

1 TABLESPOON (½ OUNCE) GRENADINE (PAGE 23)

GARNISHES: ORANGE SLICE, MARASCHINO CHERRY

When Keith Richards of the Rolling Stones ordered a margarita at The Trident bar in the seaside town of Sausalito, California, in the early 70s, bartender Bobby Lozoff shook up this concoction instead. While it may have been The Eagles who crooned "Just Another Tequila Sunrise," it was the Stones who took this ombre-hued, three-ingredient cocktail on the road to infamy.

SERVES 1

Pour the orange juice and tequila over ice in a highball glass; add Grenadine. Do not stir. Garnish, if desired.

el diablo

(COCKTAIL ON LEFT)

1 TABLESPOON (½ OUNCE) FRESH LIME JUICE

1 TABLESPOON (½ OUNCE) CRÈME DE CASSIS

3 TABLESPOONS (1½ OUNCES) REPOSADO OR AÑEJO TEQUILA

⅓ CUP (ABOUT 2½ OUNCES) GINGER BEER OR GINGER ALE

GARNISHES: LIME SLICE, SLICED FRESH GINGER

This Trader Vic's cocktail from the 40s is a blushing tequila spin on today's trendy Moscow Mule. A dash of crème de cassis, French black currant liqueur, adds a touch of sweetness and lends the drink a devilish color. The complex flavor of aged reposado tequila is a good match for ginger beer's assertive flavor. Reposado is aged in wood barrels that lend a mellow character to the liquor. Be aware that some versions contain added flavorings and colorings. See page 41 for more about tequila.

SERVES 1

Combine the first 4 ingredients in an ice-filled cocktail shaker, and shake vigorously. Strain into an ice-filled highball glass. Garnish, if desired.

Tequila

LIKE CHAMPAGNE, tequila gets its name from its region of origin. This spirit of Aztec beginnings and Spanish refinement is produced in the Mexican state of Jalisco, which includes the city of Tequila. The liquor is distilled solely from blue agave plants, which grow in the red volcanic lowland soil and the darker, richer soil of the highlands. Tequila from lowland agaves has a more pungent, earthy flavor, while highland Tequila has a sweeter finish.

BLANCO (white): Blanco, the purest of the tequila types, is typically bottled immediately after distillation. Blanco has a sharper burn than its aged counterparts, but it also has a striking agave taste—especially when made with 100% agave.

PLATA (silver): Like blanco tequila, plata is clear in color and rarely aged longer than a few weeks. Plata tequila is most commonly used in mixed drinks, such as margaritas.

ORO (gold): Oro stands out because of its golden hue, but the color usually comes from caramel coloring added to blanco or plata tequila. Look for oro tequilas made with 100% agave—these are better quality and contain fewer artificial additives.

JOVEN (young): Like oro tequila, joven starts as blanco tequila ("young" because it is not aged), and then is blended with reposado tequila for a richer, mellower taste.

REPOSADO (rested): As its name hints, reposado tequila is "rested," or aged, for up to one year in wooden barrels. Reposado has a golden hue that darkens depending on its age. The longer the tequila rests, the more mellow and rich it becomes—but it still keeps the distinctive agave flavor.

chalino special

(COCKTAIL AT TOP)

What differentiates this Prohibition-era tequila cocktail from an El Diablo is the lack of ginger beer and a duo of citrus juices. That both recipes call for a splash of sweet French liqueur may seem odd, but the stateside bartenders who created the drinks looked for ways to temper tequila's bite in order to cater to American tastes of the time. For a sweeter cocktail, add the Simple Syrup.

SERVES 1

Combine the first 4 ingredients and, if desired, the Simple Syrup in an ice-filled cocktail shaker, and shake vigorously. Strain into a martini glass. Garnish, if desired.

1	TABLESPOON (½ OUNCE) FRESH LIME JUICE
1	TABLESPOON (½ OUNCE) FRESH LEMON JUICE
3	TABLESPOONS (1½ OUNCES) WHITE TEQUILA
1½	TEASPOONS (¼ OUNCE) CHAMBORD OR CRÈME DE CASSIS
½	TEASPOON (ABOUT ⅙ OUNCE) SIMPLE SYRUP (PAGE 17) (OPTIONAL)

GARNISH: LEMON OR LIME ZEST TWIST

matador

(COCKTAIL AT BOTTOM)

Pineapple juice infuses this tequila tipple with true tropical flavor.

SERVES 1

Combine the first 3 ingredients and, if desired, the Simple Syrup in an ice-filled cocktail shaker, and shake vigorously. Strain into an ice-filled rocks glass. Garnish, if desired.

1	TABLESPOON (½ OUNCE) FRESH LIME JUICE
3	TABLESPOONS (1½ OUNCES) WHITE TEQUILA
¼	CUP (2 OUNCES) UNSWEETENED PINEAPPLE JUICE
½	TEASPOON (ABOUT ⅙ OUNCE) SIMPLE SYRUP (PAGE 17) (OPTIONAL)

GARNISHES: PINEAPPLE CHUNK, LIME WEDGE

the coastal margarita

(COCKTAIL SHOWN)

CITRUS RIM SALT (PAGE 32) OR
    COARSE SALT

LIME WEDGE

2   TABLESPOONS (1 OUNCE)
    SILVER TEQUILA

2   TABLESPOONS (1 OUNCE)
    COINTREAU

2   TABLESPOONS (1 OUNCE) FRESH
    KEY LIME JUICE (ABOUT 3 KEY
    LIMES)

1   TEASPOON (ABOUT ⅛ OUNCE)
    AGAVE NECTAR OR SIMPLE
    SYRUP (PAGE 17)

GARNISH: LIME WEDGES

Agave is a perfectly compatible sweetener for tequila cocktails. We especially like the tartness of Key limes in our signature margarita. Serve chilled neat or on the rocks.

SERVES 1

1 For a salt-rimmed margarita, pour the salt on a shallow plate. Rub rim of a chilled margarita glass with lime wedge, and twist rim of glass in salt.

2 Fill a cocktail shaker half full with ice. Add the tequila and next 3 ingredients, and shake vigorously until thoroughly chilled. Strain into prepared glass. Garnish, if desired.

mango margaritas

¾ CUP (6 OUNCES) FRESH
    ORANGE JUICE (ABOUT 3
    ORANGES)

1   LARGE MANGO, SEEDED AND
    CHOPPED

¼ CUP (2 OUNCES) FRESH
    KEY LIME JUICE (ABOUT
    6 KEY LIMES)

⅓ CUP (ABOUT 2½ OUNCES)
    SILVER TEQUILA

¼ CUP (2 OUNCES) COINTREAU OR
    OTHER ORANGE LIQUEUR

¼ CUP (2 OUNCES) SIMPLE SYRUP
    (PAGE 17)

Fresh mango blends deliciously with tequila and Cointreau in this frosty margarita. When blending frozen margaritas, there is no sense making each drink to order, so this recipe yields a small batch. Store any unused portion in the freezer.

SERVES 4

Combine all the ingredients in a blender, cover with lid, and process until smooth. Add ice to make 4 cups; process until smooth.

VARIATION:

minty mango margaritas: Add ¼ cup loosely packed fresh mint leaves, and substitute Mint Simple Syrup (page 17) for the plain Simple Syrup before blending.

CALIFORNIA

In California, sips and sand go together like sea and sun. Surfside bars span from the tip to the top of the Golden State.

silver monk

If the margarita is the Hollywood star of the beach bar menu, the Silver Monk is its sophisticated, saltier brother. Both drinks call for tequila, simple syrup and lime juice, but the Silver Monk stands apart because it adds salt into the mix rather than rimming the glass. Its name is a nod to the French Carthusian monks who make the herbaceous Chartreuse that gives the drink its verdant hue.

SERVES 1

Muddle the mint sprig, 3 of the cucumber slices, Simple Syrup, and salt in the bottom of a cocktail shaker for 30 seconds. Add tequila, Chartreuse, lime juice, and ice to fill shaker. Cover with lid, and shake vigorously for 30 seconds. Strain into a chilled coupe glass. Garnish with remaining cucumber slices.

1   FRESH MINT SPRIG

6   THIN ENGLISH CUCUMBER
    SLICES

2   TABLESPOONS SIMPLE SYRUP
    (PAGE 17)

⅛   TEASPOON KOSHER SALT

3   TABLESPOONS (1½ OUNCES)
    BLANCO TEQUILA

1   TABLESPOON (½ OUNCE) GREEN
    CHARTREUSE

½   TABLESPOON FRESH LIME JUICE

paloma

Mexico's beloved cocktail may be made with smoky mescal or tequila. Do not stir before serving for a layered ombre look in the glass.

KOSHER SALT OR CITRUS RIM SALT
  (PAGE 32)

LIME WEDGE

¼   CUP (2 OUNCES) SILVER OR
    WHITE TEQUILA OR MESCAL

1   TABLESPOON (½ OUNCE) FRESH
    LIME JUICE

⅓   CUP (ABOUT 2½ OUNCES)
    FRESH PINK GRAPEFRUIT JUICE
    (FROM 1 GRAPEFRUIT)

1   TEASPOON (ABOUT ⅛ OUNCE)
    SIMPLE SYRUP (PAGE 17)

CLUB SODA OR GRAPEFRUIT SODA

GARNISHES: GRAPEFRUIT WEDGE,
  LIME SLICE

SERVES 1

1 For a salt-rimmed cocktail, pour the salt on a shallow plate. Rub the rim of a chilled highball glass with lime wedge, and twist the rim of the glass in the salt.

2 Combine the tequila or mescal, lime juice, pink grapefruit juice, and Simple Syrup in the prepared ice-filled glass. Top off with club soda or grapefruit soda. Garnish, if desired.

A beach bum and golfer's paradise, Cabo is at the tip of Mexico's Baja California Peninsula.

Rum & Cachaça

RUM MAY BE THE LIBATION OF CHOICE for the swashbuckler in all of us, but its close cousin, cachaça, should not be overlooked. Though sweet sugarcane serves as the foundation for both drinks, their distillation processes differ: Cachaça is made from the juice of fresh sugarcane, and rum is usually made from molasses, the syrupy by-product of boiled sugar.

While rum and cachaça share a common ingredient base, the origins of the alcohols are murkier. European colonizers—mainly from Portugal—oversaw successful sugarcane plantations in Brazil and the Caribbean islands in the 16th century, and cachaça was reportedly first distilled in Brazil during that time period. Today, cachaça remains the national drink of Brazil, and it can be distilled and bottled only in its home country. Conversely, rum's founding nation is a mystery. Legends claim that plantation slaves in Barbados first began fermenting molasses in the mid-17th century, producing the original rum. However, other records suggest Brazil distilled rum much earlier, in the 1620s. Today, rum is produced widely across the Americas, but it still retains its tropical roots.

Because of its raw sugarcane base, cachaça tends to have a grassy, earthy quality to it. Rum, generally the sweeter of the two, is rounded with notes of vanilla and caramel. Light (unaged) and dark (aged) versions of both cachaça and rum can be purchased, and they are popular in different drinks: Traditionally, light versions of rum and cachaça are used in fruit-based cocktails, such as daiquiris and mojitos, while darker versions are served on the rocks or used in drinks such as Bermuda's Dark 'n' Stormy. Caipirinha, the national cocktail of Brazil, and perhaps the most famous cachaça-based drink, can be made with either dark or light cachaça—both versions mix beautifully with sugar and limes, the treasured exports of Brazil.

caipirinha

The national drink of Brazil uses cachaça, the rumlike liquor made from sugarcane. It is a muddled drink, like a mint julep, only with lime and sugar instead of mint and sugar. Bruising the lime quarters and sugar with a pestle or the back of a spoon releases flavorful oils and juice from the rind of the fruit and gives the cocktail its fresh, bright flavor.

SERVES 1

Combine the lime quarters and sugar in a cocktail shaker. Muddle until juices have released and sugar is mostly dissolved. Add the crushed ice and cachaça; cover and shake vigorously until thoroughly chilled. Pour contents of shaker into a chilled rocks glass. Garnish, if desired.

½   LIME, CUT INTO QUARTERS

1   TO 2 TEASPOONS SUPERFINE SUGAR

½   CUP CRUSHED ICE

¼   CUP (2 OUNCES) CACHAÇA (BRAZILIAN SUGARCANE LIQUOR)

GARNISHES: STARFRUIT SLICE, LIME QUARTERS, SUGARCANE SWIZZLE STICK

Bar Talk

MUDDLE—

THE PROCESS OF CRUSHING INGREDIENTS IN THE BOTTOM OF A GLASS WITH A SPOON OR MUDDLER TO RELEASE THE FLAVORFUL ESSENCE INTO THE COCKTAIL.

classic daiquiri

¼ CUP (2 OUNCES) FLOR DE CAÑA WHITE RUM

1½ TABLESPOONS (¾ OUNCE) FRESH LIME JUICE

1½ TABLESPOONS (¾ OUNCE) SIMPLE SYRUP (PAGE 17)

GARNISH: THIN LIME SLICE

Use this three-ingredient recipe from barkeep Ingi Sigurdsson at the Jack Dusty restaurant at The Ritz-Carlton, Sarasota, Florida, to prepare a refreshing daiquiri.

SERVES 1

Combine the first 3 ingredients in an ice-filled cocktail shaker, and shake vigorously for 30 seconds or until well chilled. Strain into a Champagne coupe or martini glass. Garnish, if desired.

the pink daiquiri

(COCKTAIL SHOWN)

3 TABLESPOONS (1½ OUNCES) WHITE RUM

1½ TEASPOONS (ABOUT ¼ OUNCE) MARASCHINO LIQUEUR (SUCH AS LUXARDO MARASCHINO)

1 TABLESPOON (½ OUNCE) FRESH LEMON JUICE

2 TABLESPOONS (1 OUNCE) FRESH RUBY RED GRAPEFRUIT JUICE

1 TABLESPOON (½ OUNCE) SIMPLE SYRUP (PAGE 17)

GARNISH: GRAPEFRUIT WEDGE

The original daiquiri contained rum, fresh lime juice, and sugar. Ernest Hemingway is credited with the addition of maraschino liqueur and grapefruit juice.

SERVES 1

Combine the first 5 ingredients in an ice-filled cocktail shaker, and shake vigorously. Strain into a chilled coupe glass. Garnish, if desired.

minty lime frozen mojito

(COCKTAIL FAR LEFT, PAGE 56)

Refreshingly dangerous and perfectly fitting for seaside sipping, this mojito doubles easily. Keep batches in the freezer until you're ready to imbibe.

SERVES 3

1 (6-OUNCE) CAN FROZEN LIMEADE CONCENTRATE

¾ CUP (6 OUNCES) LIGHT RUM

⅓ CUP LOOSELY PACKED FRESH MINT LEAVES

GARNISHES: FRESH MINT SPRIGS, LIME WEDGES

Combine first 3 ingredients in a blender. Add crushed ice to make 5 cups; cover with lid, and process until smooth. Garnish, if desired.

tortola mojito

(COCKTAIL FAR RIGHT, PAGE 57)

Muddling releases flavorful oils from the citrus and herbs. Infused rum is easy to make and adds uncommon flavor to cocktails.

SERVES 1

2 LIME SLICES

1 TEASPOON LIGHT BROWN SUGAR OR LEMONGRASS SIMPLE SYRUP (PAGE 17)

2 FRESH BASIL LEAVES

3 TABLESPOONS (1½ OUNCES) BASIL-LEMONGRASS RUM OR WHITE RUM

½ CUP (4 OUNCES) GINGER BEER

GARNISHES: LIME SLICES, FRESH BASIL OR MINT LEAVES, FRESH LEMONGRASS, BLOSSOMS

1 Place the lime slices in an old-fashioned or rocks glass; add sugar or syrup and basil. Crush with a muddler or wooden spoon until fruit and basil leaves are bruised and sugar, if using, dissolves.

2 Fill glass with ice, and top off with Basil-Lemongrass Rum or white rum and ginger beer. Garnish, if desired.

basil-lemongrass rum: Pour about 3 tablespoons rum out of a 750-milliliter bottle. Add 2 crushed fresh lemongrass stalks, 1 bunch basil, and 1 lemon rind (white pith scraped away). Steep in the bottle at least 1 week. Makes about 3 cups

cranberry mojito

(COCKTAIL CENTER, PAGE 57)

Fresh cranberries, mint, and lime slices add a holiday vibe to the classic mojito.

SERVES 1

Muddle the first 4 ingredients in a tall glass. Add ice, rum, and sparkling water, and stir gently. Garnish, if desired.

- ½ LIME, CUT INTO 4 WEDGES
- ¼ CUP (2 OUNCES) FRESH CRANBERRIES OR FROZEN CRANBERRIES, THAWED
- 2 TABLESPOONS FRESH MINT LEAVES
- 2 TABLESPOONS SUGAR
- 3 TABLESPOONS (1½ OUNCES) LIGHT RUM
- ½ CUP (4 OUNCES) SPARKLING WATER

GARNISHES: LIME ZEST TWIST, LIME SLICES, FRESH CRANBERRIES, FRESH MINT LEAVES, ORCHID BLOSSOM

coconut mojito

(COCKTAIL SECOND FROM RIGHT, PAGE 57)

Escape to the tropics with this beachy cocktail from the Scarlet Bistro on the Barbados coast.

SERVES 1

1 Muddle the 6 mint leaves, 3 lime wedges, and brown sugar in the bottom of a cocktail shaker. Add the white rum, coconut rum, and cream of coconut.

2 Fill cocktail shaker with ice, and stir vigorously until chilled. Strain into a tall glass, and top off with chilled club soda. Garnish, if desired.

- 6 FRESH MINT LEAVES
- 3 LIME WEDGES
- 1 TEASPOON BROWN SUGAR
- 2½ TABLESPOONS (1¼ OUNCES) MOUNT GAY WHITE RUM
- 1 TABLESPOON (½ OUNCE) MALIBU COCONUT RUM
- 2 TABLESPOONS (1 OUNCE) CREAM OF COCONUT
- 1 CUP (8 OUNCES) CLUB SODA, CHILLED

GARNISHES: COCONUT SLICE, FRESH MINT SPRIG

the drunken sailor

Dry 85 in Annapolis uses locally distilled rum in its version of this nautical classic, a perfect boating cocktail with make-ahead mint-infused simple syrup.

SERVES 1

Combine Mint Simple Syrup and rum in a cocktail shaker, and shake until combined. Strain into an ice-filled copper mug. Top off with ginger beer. Garnish, if desired.

¼ CUP (2 OUNCES) MINT SIMPLE SYRUP (PAGE 17)

¼ CUP (2 OUNCES) BARREL-AGED RUM OR WHITE RUM

GINGER BEER (SUCH AS FEVER TREE)

GARNISHES: LIME SLICE, CRYSTALLIZED GINGER

Bar Talk

COPPER CUPS—
A MUST-HAVE FOR SERVING A CLASSIC MOSCOW MULE, COPPER'S CONDUCTIVENESS AMPLIFIES THE CHILL OF ANY DRINK WHILE IT'S SIPPED.

Perennially popular
Kapalua Beach in Maui,
Hawaii, offers some of
the best snorkeling on
the island.

mai tai

(COCKTAIL BACK CENTER)

2 TABLESPOONS (1 OUNCE) LIGHT
  RUM

2 TABLESPOONS (1 OUNCE)
  CURAÇAO

2 TABLESPOONS (1 OUNCE) FRESH
  ORANGE JUICE

1 TABLESPOON (½ OUNCE) FRESH
  LIME JUICE

½ TEASPOON (ABOUT ⅟₁₆ OUNCE)
  TOASTED ORGEAT SYRUP
  (PAGE 20)

½ TEASPOON (ABOUT ⅟₁₆ OUNCE)
  SIMPLE SYRUP (PAGE 17)

½ TABLESPOON (¼ OUNCE) DARK
  RUM

GARNISHES: FRESH MINT SPRIG,
  LIME WEDGE, PINEAPPLE SLICE

Both Victor Bergeron of Trader Vic's and Donn Beach of Don the Beachcomber took credit for creating this quintessential tiki cocktail. Versions containing pineapple juice are typically credited to Victor, who was commissioned to develop a signature spin on the mai tai cocktail for the Royal Hawaiian Hotel. This recipe skews closer to the mai tai of questionable origin.

SERVES 1

Pour the first 6 ingredients into an ice-filled highball glass. Drizzle dark rum on top. Garnish, if desired.

missionary's downfall

(COCKTAIL FRONT CENTER, PAGE 65)

1 FRESH PEACH SLICE, PLUS 2 FOR GARNISH

1 TABLESPOON PEACH PRESERVES

1 TABLESPOON FRESH PINEAPPLE JUICE

1 FRESH MINT SPRIG, PLUS 1 FOR GARNISH

3 TABLESPOONS (1½ OUNCES) WHITE RUM

1 TABLESPOON HONEY

⅛ TEASPOON KOSHER SALT

As its name implies, this tiki bar classic is hard to turn down. The Downfall strikes a perfect blend of sweet and refreshing, combining honey with fresh pineapple and crisp mint leaves.

SERVES 1

Muddle 1 peach slice, peach preserves, pineapple juice, and 1 mint sprig in the bottom of a cocktail shaker 30 seconds. Add the rum, honey, and salt to cocktail shaker. Fill with ice; cover with lid, and shake vigorously 30 seconds. Strain into a chilled rocks glass filled with ice. Garnish with a mint sprig and 2 peach slices.

navy grog

(COCKTAIL FAR LEFT, PAGE 65)

2 TABLESPOONS (1 OUNCE) DARK RUM

2 TABLESPOONS (1 OUNCE) LIGHT RUM

1 TABLESPOON GINGER-HONEY SYRUP (PAGE 18) OR SIMPLE SYRUP (PAGE 17)

1 TABLESPOON FRESH LIME JUICE

1 ICE CONE

Rumor has it that when the Navy Grog was first served in Hollywood, Frank Sinatra claimed it as his favorite drink. Chances are, Frank would've liked it even more on the beach. Traditionally made with three types of rum, the Grog is no small drink—but sipping it through a frozen snow cone makes it a little more fun.

SERVES 1

Combine the rums, Ginger-Honey Syrup, and lime juice in a cocktail shaker. Fill with ice; cover with lid, and shake vigorously 30 seconds. Place frozen ice cone, pointing up, in a chilled rocks glass. Strain drink mixture over frozen ice cone or crushed ice.

ICE CONE: Firmly pack finely crushed ice into the bottom half of a 7-ounce plastic-lined paper cone. Pour in just enough water to cover ice. Place, upright, in a narrow freezer-safe glass, and freeze until completely firm, about 8 hours. Tear paper from frozen ice cone and use immediately.

test pilot

(COCKTAIL SECOND FROM RIGHT, PAGE 65)

For the drinker who's skeptical about tiki libations, the Test Pilot is the perfect introduction. Along with Don the Beachcomber's traditional rum base, angostura bitters and Falernum Syrup add a spicy kick to each sip.

SERVES 1

Combine all the ingredients in a blender, and process until mostly smooth. Pour into a double old-fashioned glass, adding more crushed ice, if necessary.

1   CUP CRUSHED ICE

¼   CUP (2 OUNCES) WHITE RUM

1   TABLESPOON (½ OUNCE) FALERNUM SYRUP (PAGE 20)

1   TABLESPOON (½ OUNCE) ORANGE LIQUEUR (SUCH AS GRAND MARNIER)

1   TABLESPOON FRESH LIME JUICE

6   DROPS OF PERNOD (ANISE LIQUEUR)

1   DASH OF ANGOSTURA BITTERS

bahama hurricane

(COCKTAIL FAR RIGHT, PAGE 65)

A standard in bars in Nassau, this rendition of the hurricane is nothing like New Orleans' potent punch. Consider this a chilled eye-opener of a cocktail that is a fine restorative after a bitter tropical storm or as a delicious post-meal digestif.

SERVES 1

Combine all the ingredients in a cocktail shaker filled with ice. Cover and shake vigorously until chilled, about 30 seconds. Strain into an ice-filled hurricane glass or other tall glass. Garnish, if desired.

¼   CUP (2 OUNCES) 151-PROOF RUM

2   TABLESPOONS (1 OUNCE) COFFEE LIQUEUR

2   TABLESPOONS (1 OUNCE) IRISH CREAM LIQUEUR (SUCH AS BAILEYS)

1   TEASPOON ORANGE LIQUEUR

GARNISHES: ORANGE WEDGES, COCKTAIL UMBRELLA

passion fruit zombie

Tropical fruit and apricot brandy give this drink a balanced sweetness, tempered by tart lime juice and a dash of bitters. The zombie is a strong and sweet cocktail—especially with the dark rum topper—that has made many an imbiber feel like a zombie the morning after. Drink slowly with caution!

SERVES 1

Combine the first 4 ingredients in an ice-filled cocktail shaker, and shake vigorously. Strain into an ice-filled rocks glass. Top off with dark rum, if desired. Garnish, if desired.

zombie mix

2   CUPS (16 OUNCES) FRESH PINEAPPLE JUICE

1   CUP (8 OUNCES) PASSION FRUIT JUICE OR NECTAR

1   CUP (8 OUNCES) APRICOT BRANDY (SUCH AS MARIE BRIZARD APRY)

½   CUP (4 OUNCES) FRESH LIME JUICE (ABOUT 4 LIMES)

¼   CUP (2 OUNCES) GRENADINE (PAGE 23)

Combine all the ingredients in a large jar; stir until blended. Makes 4¾ cups (enough for 10 cocktails)

1½ TABLESPOONS (¾ OUNCE) GOLD RUM

1½ TABLESPOONS (¾ OUNCE) SILVER OR WHITE RUM

½   CUP (4 OUNCES) ZOMBIE MIX

1   DASH ANGOSTURA BITTERS OR HOMEMADE PEACH-VANILLA BITTERS (PAGE 27)

½   TO 1 TABLESPOON (¼ TO ½ OUNCE) DARK RUM (OPTIONAL)

GARNISHES: MARASCHINO CHERRY, COCKTAIL UMBRELLA

JAMAICA

The third largest island of the Caribbean is made up of mountains, forests, waterfalls, lagoons, and coral reefs.

planter's punch

South Carolina's Planter's Inn often takes credit for this tiki cocktail, but it first appeared in print in 1895 in the book Modern American Drinks *as Jamaican Rum Punch. Call it what you may—we call it delicious!*

- 1½ CUPS CRUSHED ICE OR 6 ICE CUBES
- ½ CUP (4 OUNCES) CHILLED FRESH PINEAPPLE JUICE
- ¼ CUP (2 OUNCES) CHILLED FRESH ORANGE JUICE
- ¼ CUP (2 OUNCES) CHILLED FRESH LIME JUICE (ABOUT 2 LIMES)
- ¼ CUP (2 OUNCES) DARK RUM

GRENADINE (PAGE 23)

GARNISHES: MARASCHINO CHERRIES, ORANGE SLICES, PINEAPPLE WEDGE, COCKTAIL UMBRELLA

SERVES 1

Fill a cocktail shaker with ice, and add juices and rum. Shake vigorously to blend. Strain into a highball glass. Top off with a splash of Grenadine. Garnish, if desired.

cuba libre

The authentic name for a rum and cola, this cocktail was created as a curative. For what, you ask? How about whatever ails you?

SERVES 1

1 Squeeze the juice from the lime into a Collins glass. Drop the lime half in the glass, and muddle with a muddler to bruise and extract some of the oils from the rind.
2 Fill glass with ice. Pour rum over the ice, and top off with cola. Garnish, if desired.

½   LIME
¼   CUP (2 OUNCES) DARK RUM
½   CUP (4 OUNCES) COLA
GARNISH: LIME WEDGE

rum runner

The story goes that this Key West cocktail was created in the 1950s at the Holiday Isle Tiki Bar in Islamorada, Florida. It was named for the bootleggers who smuggled in the liquor during Prohibition and later to avoid taxes. There's nothing taxing about this decidedly tropical rum-and-liqueur–packed libation.

SERVES 1

Pour all ingredients into an ice-filled cocktail shaker, and shake vigorously. Strain into an ice-filled hurricane glass. Garnish, if desired.

2   TABLESPOONS (1 OUNCE) FRESH LIME JUICE
2   TABLESPOONS (1 OUNCE) FRESH ORANGE JUICE
2   TABLESPOONS (1 OUNCE) UNSWEETENED PINEAPPLE JUICE
2   TABLESPOONS (1 OUNCE) BANANA LIQUEUR
2   TABLESPOONS (1 OUNCE) LIGHT RUM
2   TABLESPOONS (1 OUNCE) DARK RUM
1   TABLESPOON (½ OUNCE) CHAMBORD
1   TABLESPOON (½ OUNCE) GRENADINE (PAGE 23)
GARNISH: FRUIT SKEWER (PINEAPPLE, BANANA, ORANGE, LIME)

chartreuse swizzle

(COCKTAIL SHOWN)

Most swizzles have a rum base. Green chartreuse, an herbal liqueur that pairs perfectly with lime and pineapple, spikes this swizzle.

SERVES 1

1   CUP CRUSHED ICE

3   TABLESPOONS (1½ OUNCES) GREEN CHARTREUSE

2   TABLESPOONS UNSWEETENED PINEAPPLE JUICE

1½ TABLESPOONS FRESH LIME JUICE

1   TABLESPOON (½ OUNCE) FALERNUM SYRUP (PAGE 20)

GARNISHES: FRESH MINT LEAVES, GRATED FRESH NUTMEG

Combine the crushed ice, Green Chartreuse, pineapple juice, lime juice, and Falernum Syrup in a Collins glass. Stir until frost appears on outside of glass. Top with more crushed ice, if necessary. Garnish, if desired.

caribbean rum swizzle

This mixture of rum and fruit juices gets its name from the forked allspice or sassafras branch used to stir it.

SERVES 1

1   TABLESPOON (½ OUNCE) GOSLINGS BLACK SEAL RUM

1   TABLESPOON (½ OUNCE) GOSLINGS GOLD RUM

¼   CUP (2 OUNCES) UNSWEETENED PINEAPPLE JUICE

¼   CUP (2 OUNCES) FRESH ORANGE JUICE

1½ TABLESPOONS (¾ OUNCE) GRENADINE (PAGE 23)

1   TABLESPOON (½ OUNCE) FALERNUM SYRUP (PAGE 20)

2   DASHES OF ANGOSTURA BITTERS

GARNISH: SWIZZLE STICK-SKEWERED PINEAPPLE

Pour the first 7 ingredients into an ice-filled highball glass. Stir vigorously until foamy. Garnish, if desired, and stir cocktail often while drinking.

Bar Talk

SWIZZLE—

THIS BERMUDA BEVERAGE HAS A FUZZY PROVENANCE, BUT IT IS THE INSPIRATION FOR THE SWIZZLE STICK USED TO STIR IT.

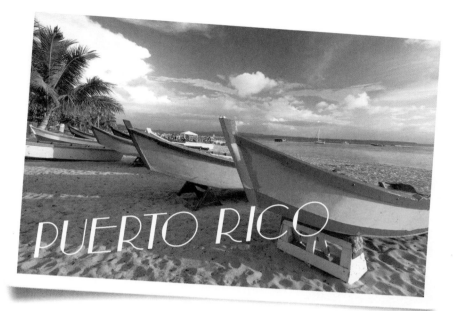

The largest insular territory of the United States is a multi-island archipelago.

piña colada

Skip the store-bought colada mix and whip up your own with chopped fresh pineapple, rum, fresh lime juice, cream of coconut, and pineapple juice. The optional black strap rum adds a distinctive molasses note, as its name suggests, and a complexity that ups the flavor ante of this classic tiki cocktail.

SERVES 2

Combine first 6 ingredients in a blender, cover with lid, and process until smooth. Pour into 2 Collins glasses. Top off each with additional 1½ teaspoons (¼ ounce) black strap rum, if desired. Garnish, if desired.

- ½ CUP CHOPPED FRESH PINEAPPLE
- 6 TABLESPOONS (3 OUNCES) SILVER OR WHITE RUM
- 3 TABLESPOONS (1½ OUNCES) FRESH LIME JUICE
- 6 TABLESPOONS (3 OUNCES) CREAM OF COCONUT
- ¼ CUP (2 OUNCES) FRESH PINEAPPLE JUICE
- 3 CUPS ICE CUBES
- 1 TABLESPOON (½ OUNCE) BLACK STRAP RUM (OPTIONAL)

GARNISHES: FRESH PINEAPPLE WEDGES, FRESH MINT SPRIGS

the saturn

1   CUP CRUSHED ICE

2½ TABLESPOONS (1¼ OUNCES) GIN

1   TABLESPOON FRESH LEMON
    JUICE

1   TABLESPOON PASSION FRUIT
    NECTAR

1½ TEASPOONS (¼ OUNCE)
    FALERNUM SYRUP (PAGE 20)

1½ TEASPOONS (¼ OUNCE)
    TOASTED ORGEAT SYRUP
    (PAGE 20)

GARNISH: LEMON ZEST TWIST

Saturn steps out at the tiki bar as a gin-based drink. Although rum is absent, the mix still boasts the flavors of a classic beach cocktail: Passion fruit, citrus juice, orgeat, and falernum shine through this light sipper.

SERVES 1

Process the crushed ice, gin, lemon juice, nectar, falernum, and orgeat in a blender until smooth. Pour into a Collins glass. Garnish, if desired.

singapore sling
(COCKTAIL SHOWN)

2   TABLESPOONS UNSWEETENED
    PINEAPPLE JUICE

1½ TABLESPOONS (¾ OUNCE) GIN

1   TABLESPOON FRESH LIME JUICE

1½ TEASPOONS (¼ OUNCE)
    ORANGE LIQUEUR (SUCH AS
    GRAND MARNIER)

1½ TEASPOONS (¼ OUNCE) CHERRY
    LIQUEUR (SUCH AS HEERING)

1½ TEASPOONS (¼ OUNCE)
    HERBAL LIQUEUR (SUCH AS
    BÉNÉDICTINE)

1   DASH OF HOMEMADE PEACH-
    VANILLA BITTERS (PAGE 27)

¼   CUP CLUB SODA

GARNISHES: ORANGE SLICES,
    MARASCHINO CHERRIES

First crafted at the Long Bar in the Raffles Hotel in Singapore in the early 1900s, the Singapore Sling is known for its bright pink hue and foamy fruit punch cap. The drink combines gin, cherry brandy, and citrus juices for a sweet treat. Sling comes from the German "schlingen" meaning to swallow and refers to spirits diluted with water or soda.

SERVES 1

Combine the pineapple juice, gin, lime juice, orange liqueur, cherry liqueur, herbal liqueur, and bitters in a cocktail shaker filled with ice. Cover and shake vigorously until thoroughly chilled, about 15 seconds. Strain into a highball glass. Top with the club soda, and garnish, if desired.

fog cutter

(COCKTAIL ON RIGHT)

Another of Trader Vic's classic concoctions, the Fog Cutter pairs rum with brandy and gin for a strong (ahem, fog-cutting) punch. Lemon juice and orange juice brighten the blow.

SERVES 1

Combine the orange juice, rum, lemon juice, gin, brandy, and syrup in a cocktail shaker filled with ice. Cover and shake vigorously until chilled, about 30 seconds. Strain into a highball glass filled with ice. Top with sherry. Gently slap mint sprig against your wrist to release oils, and place mint sprig in glass. Garnish, if desired.

¼ CUP FRESH ORANGE JUICE

3 TABLESPOONS (1½ OUNCES) WHITE RUM

2 TABLESPOONS FRESH LEMON JUICE

1 TABLESPOON (½ OUNCE) DRY GIN

1 TABLESPOON (½ OUNCE) BRANDY

1 TABLESPOON TOASTED ORGEAT SYRUP (PAGE 20)

1 TABLESPOON (½ OUNCE) AMONTILLADO SHERRY

MINT SPRIG

GARNISH: ORCHID BLOSSOM, FRESH ORANGE SLICE

royal hawaiian

(COCKTAIL ON LEFT)

For a lighter spin on tiki drinks, the Royal Hawaiian packs the flavor you want without the sugar load. The gin-and-pineapple drink was first crafted in the 1920s at the Royal Hawaiian Hotel, one of the first hotels in Waikiki.

SERVES 1

1 Freeze a martini glass 1 hour.
2 Combine the first 4 ingredients in a cocktail shaker filled with ice. Cover and shake vigorously until chilled, about 30 seconds. Strain into frozen martini glass. Garnish, if desired. Serve immediately.

3 TABLESPOONS (1½ OUNCES) GIN

2 TABLESPOONS FRESH UNSWEETENED PINEAPPLE JUICE

1½ TABLESPOONS TOASTED ORGEAT SYRUP (PAGE 20)

1 TABLESPOON FRESH LEMON JUICE

GARNISHES; FRESH PINEAPPLE WEDGES, BLOSSOMS

blue hawaiian

⅓ CUP (ABOUT 2½ OUNCES) PINEAPPLE VODKA

2 TABLESPOONS (1 OUNCE) BLUE CURAÇAO

2 TABLESPOONS (1 OUNCE) COCONUT RUM

1 TABLESPOON (½ OUNCE) AMARETTO

2 TABLESPOONS (1 OUNCE) FRESH LIME JUICE

¼ CUP (2 OUNCES) AGAVE NECTAR, SIMPLE SYRUP (PAGE 17), OR SUGAR

4 CUPS ICE CUBES

GARNISHES: FRESH PINEAPPLE CHUNKS, MARASCHINO CHERRIES, LIME SLICES

Curaçao, a liqueur flavored with peels of laraha citrus fruit, was first bottled on the Caribbean island of Curaçao. The island's arid climate cannot support sweet Valencia oranges, but bitter, nearly inedible larahas grow in abundance. When dried, lahara peels emit sweet oils, which tinge the liqueur with orange-like flavor. Although it's naturally colorless, curaçao is often dyed blue for tropical drinks.

SERVES 4

Combine first 7 ingredients in blender, cover with lid, and process until smooth. Pour into hurricane glasses. Garnish, if desired.

chi chi

½ (13.5-OUNCE) CAN (7½ OUNCES) COCONUT MILK

6 (1-INCH) CUBES FRESH PINEAPPLE

¾ CUP (6 OUNCES) VODKA

3 CUPS CRUSHED ICE

GARNISHES: STAR FRUIT SLICES, ORNAMENTAL PINEAPPLES

Like a piña colada, only made with vodka, this creamy cocktail is a substantial summer refresher.

SERVES 4

Combine first 4 ingredients in a blender, cover with lid, and process until smooth, stopping to scrape down sides. Garnish, if desired. Serve immediately.

VARIATION:

go go: Substitute fresh cubed mango for the pineapple in the mix and the garnish.

Curaçao's Kleine Knip Beach is largely undeveloped with clear water perfect for snorkeling.

harpoon

(COCKTAIL FAR RIGHT, PAGE 85)

3 TABLESPOONS (1½ OUNCES)
VODKA

1 TABLESPOON (½ OUNCE)
COINTREAU OR OTHER
ORANGE LIQUEUR

1½ TABLESPOONS (¾ OUNCE)
FRESH LIME JUICE OR
LEMONGRASS-CITRUS SHRUB
SYRUP (PAGE 28)

SPLASH OF CRANBERRY JUICE

GARNISHES: SKEWERED FRESH
CRANBERRIES, LIME SLICE

This 60s era favorite was brought to imbibers everywhere on the back of the cranberry juice bottle. Better known as a Cosmo, we prefer the nautical moniker. For a change of pace swap the lime juice for a hit of tart homemade Lemongrass-Citrus Shrub Syrup (page 28).

SERVES 1

Combine the first 4 ingredients in an ice-filled cocktail shaker, and shake vigorously. Strain into a martini glass. Garnish, if desired.

cape codder

(COCKTAIL BACK LEFT, PAGE 84)

3 TABLESPOONS (1½ OUNCES)
VODKA

½ CUP (4 OUNCES) CRANBERRY
JUICE

1 TABLESPOON (½ OUNCE) FRESH
LIME JUICE

GARNISHES: LIME SLICES,
MARASCHINO CHERRY

This back-to-basics vodka and cranberry juice cocktail proves that simple is often sublime. Swap Key limes for Persian limes for a change of pace.

SERVES 1

Combine the first 3 ingredients in an ice-filled highball glass, and stir gently. Garnish, if desired.

sex on the beach

(COCKTAIL FRONT LEFT, PAGE 84)

This drink's provocative name certainly garners attention, but it's the refreshing combination of fruity flavors and vodka that has kept revelers coming back for refills for decades.

SERVES 1

Layer the first 4 ingredients in an ice-filled highball glass. Garnish, if desired.

3   TABLESPOONS (1½ OUNCES) VODKA

3   TABLESPOONS (1½ OUNCES) FRESH ORANGE JUICE

3   TABLESPOONS (1½ OUNCES) CRANBERRY JUICE

1½ TABLESPOONS (¾ OUNCE) PEACH SCHNAPPS

GARNISHES: ORANGE SLICE, MARASCHINO CHERRY, FRESH PEACH SLICES

sea breeze

(COCKTAIL FRONT RIGHT, PAGE 84)

Another refreshing vodka and tart juice medley, only this incorporates sunny grapefruit juice into the mix.

SERVES 1

Combine the first 3 ingredients in an ice-filled cocktail shaker, and shake vigorously. Strain into an ice-filled highball glass. Garnish, if desired.

VARIATION:

bay breeze: Substitute unsweetened fresh pineapple juice for the grapefruit juice.

3   TABLESPOONS (1½ OUNCES) VODKA

½   CUP (4 OUNCES) CRANBERRY JUICE

2   TABLESPOONS (1 OUNCE) FRESH GRAPEFRUIT JUICE

GARNISHES: LIME SLICES, ORCHID BLOSSOM

zesty ginger-lime cooler
(COCKTAIL ON RIGHT)

Ginger adds an exotic spiciness to this drink, while sweet honey rounds out the flavor.

SERVES 1

Combine the first 3 ingredients in an ice-filled cocktail shaker, and shake vigorously. Strain into an ice-filled tall glass. Garnish, if desired.

¼ CUP (2 OUNCES) SPICED RUM

1½ TABLESPOONS (¾ OUNCE) GINGER-HONEY SYRUP (PAGE 18)

1½ TABLESPOONS (¾ OUNCE) FRESH LIME JUICE

GARNISHES: GINGER SLICE, LIME ZEST TWIST

lemongrass-pineapple cooler
(COCKTAIL ON LEFT)

Crisp, citrusy lemongrass combines with bold, juicy pineapple in this sunny cocktail. For best results, sip on a shaded porch on a hot summer day.

SERVES 1

Combine the first 3 ingredients in an ice-filled cocktail shaker, and shake vigorously. Strain into an ice-filled tall glass. Garnish, if desired.

¼ CUP (2 OUNCES) LIGHT RUM

1½ TABLESPOONS (¾ OUNCE) LEMONGRASS SIMPLE SYRUP (PAGE 17)

2 TABLESPOONS (1 OUNCE) UNSWEETENED PINEAPPLE JUICE

GARNISHES: FRESH MINT LEAVES, PINEAPPLE SLICE, FRESH LEMONGRASS STALK

rum old fashioned

1 (1-INCH-THICK) PIECE FRESH PINEAPPLE

1 MARASCHINO CHERRY

1 TEASPOON DARK BROWN SUGAR

DASH OF ANGOSTURA BITTERS

3 TABLESPOONS (1½ OUNCES) LIGHT RUM

¼ CUP (2 OUNCES) CLUB SODA

While the classic Old Fashioned may be king, this version will send you straight to the seaside. Brown sugar and pineapple bring out the sweet tropical notes of rum, making for a heavenly island drink.

SERVES 1

1 Place the first 4 ingredients in an old-fashioned glass. Crush with a muddler or the back of a wooden spoon into a chunky pulp.

2 Fill glass with ice. Add rum and club soda. Stir until combined.

dark 'n' stormy®

(COCKTAIL SHOWN)

6 TABLESPOONS (3 OUNCES) GOSLINGS BLACK SEAL RUM

½ CUP (4 OUNCES) GOSLINGS STORMY GINGER BEER

GARNISH: LIME WEDGES

Legend has it that the Dark 'n' Stormy got its name from a sailor disembarking in Bermuda after WWI. The sailor described the drink's dark surface as the "colour of a cloud only a fool or a dead man would sail under." It is Bermuda's national cocktail.

SERVES 1

Combine the rum and beer in an ice-filled highball glass, and stir to combine. Garnish, if desired.

belladonna cocktail

(COCKTAIL ON LEFT)

This tropical drink is simpler to remember than many tropical tipples. The formula: two rums + three juices (and a splash of grenadine). Use only fresh-squeezed juices for this blend.

SERVES 1

Combine the first 5 ingredients and a splash of Grenadine in an ice-filled cocktail shaker, and stir well with a bar spoon. Strain into an ice-filled Collins glass. Garnish, if desired.

2   TABLESPOONS (1 OUNCE) GOLD RUM

2   TABLESPOONS (1 OUNCE) LIGHT RUM

2   TABLESPOONS (1 OUNCE) FRESH ORANGE JUICE

2   TABLESPOONS (1 OUNCE) FRESH GRAPEFRUIT JUICE

2   TABLESPOONS (1 OUNCE) UNSWEETENED PINEAPPLE JUICE

GRENADINE (PAGE 23)

GARNISHES: ORANGE ZEST TWIST, ORCHID BLOSSOM

banana-rum cocktail

(COCKTAIL ON RIGHT)

Like liquid Bananas Foster, this sweet cocktail is mellowed by dark rum and lime juice. Crème de banana is a liquor cabinet investment that can be used in cakes and on ice cream, too.

SERVES 4

1 Combine the sugar and water in a small saucepan. Cook over medium-high until the sugar dissolves, stirring constantly. Remove from heat, and cool completely.

2 Combine the sugar mixture, crème de banana, rum, and lime juice in a pitcher; stir to combine. Divide mixture evenly among 4 ice-filled rocks glasses. Garnish, if desired.

¼   CUP DEMERARA SUGAR

¼   CUP WATER

1   CUP (7½ OUNCES) CRÈME DE BANANA (BANANA LIQUEUR)

½   CUP PLUS 2 TABLESPOONS (5 OUNCES) DARK RUM

5   TABLESPOONS (2½ OUNCES) FRESH LIME JUICE

GARNISHES: BANANA CHIPS, BLOSSOMS

Gin & Vodka Primer

FAR FROM THE LUSH VINEYARDS of Southern Europe, in the harsh, wintery climate of 15th-century Russia, distillers were determined to make wine with what they had on hand: bushels of wheat and bags of potatoes. They called their distilled spirit "bread wine," and later, vodka, meaning "little water" because the spirit was odorless and appeared like water to the unassuming eye. Though vodka can be drunk straight, its neutral nature makes it a perfect spirit for a wide range of libations, from two-ingredient cocktails to more complex mixed drinks.

Though vodka's mild taste gives it versatility on the bar cart, gin has the advantage of adding its distinctive flavor to an array of cocktails. First produced in Holland in the early 17th century, its appearance came centuries after vodka was born, but like vodka, gin is made from distilled grain (usually corn or barley). As was the case for many distilled spirits, gin was originally marketed as a cure for ailments like stomachaches, gout, and gallstones by Dutch pharmacies. Since the original spirit was unpleasant to drink straight, chemists added juniper berries for flavor. The concoction—still considered medicinal—was administered to British soldiers during the Thirty Years' War, where it earned a new name: "Dutch Courage." Gin landed in England soon after, where it became the nation's most popular liquor.

Perhaps because of its popularity in England, gin became widely consumed in the United States. In 1911, the martini—made with equal parts gin and dry vermouth, plus a few dashes of orange bitters—was born. At the time, vodka hadn't entered mainstream America cocktail culture. In the 1970s, a British spy ordered a martini made with vodka, and James Bond's signature drink spiked vodka sales across the country. It also sparked an enduring debate about the virtue of vodka versus gin martinis. Both spirits continue to hold prominent places on today's liquor shelf, enjoyed in cocktails both shaken and stirred.

Gently swaying palms shade the meandering trail weaving through Bastimentos National Marine Park on Panama's Zapatilla Cay.

gin and coconut water

¼ CUP (2 OUNCES) GIN

½ CUP (4 OUNCES) COCONUT
WATER (SUCH AS NAKED)

1½ TEASPOONS (¼ OUNCE) FRESH
LIME JUICE

2 TO 4 DASHES OF ANGOSTURA
BITTERS

In Ernest Hemingway's posthumously published book, Islands in the Stream, *main character, Thomas Hudson, famously sips a Gin and Coconut Water. "The tall cold drink made of gin, lime juice, green coconut water, and chipped ice with just enough Angostura bitters to give it a rusty, rose color, he held the drink in the shadow so the ice would not melt while he looked out over the sea."*

SERVES 1

Pour the gin into an ice-filled rocks glass; add coconut water and lime juice. Stir until chilled. Add the Angostura bitters, 1 dash at a time, just until cocktail is a rosy color.

key lime gimlet
(COCKTAIL SHOWN)

5 TABLESPOONS (2½ OUNCES) GIN

1½ TABLESPOONS (¾ OUNCE)
FRESH KEY LIME JUICE

1 TABLESPOON (½ OUNCE) SIMPLE
SYRUP (PAGE 17)

GARNISH: KEY LIME SLICE

Key limes, indigenous to the Florida Keys, are notably smaller, seedier, juicier, and have a stronger aroma than standard limes. The zesty flavor of Key lime shines in Florida's famous Key Lime Pie, but we like it in this crisp cocktail just as much.

SERVES 1

Combine the first 3 ingredients in an ice-filled cocktail shaker, and shake vigorously. Strain into a coupe glass. Garnish, if desired.

VARIATION:

clementine gimlet: Substitute freshly squeezed clementine (or tangerine) juice for the Key lime juice.

paradise point cooler

(COCKTAIL SHOWN)

If you can't make the trip to Paradise Point in San Diego, the resort's namesake cocktail will carry you there in spirit. Fresh strawberries and sweet elderflower liqueur pack a fragrant flavor punch.

SERVES 1

1 Muddle the hulled strawberries in the bottom of a cocktail shaker with a muddler or the back of a wooden spoon.

2 Fill cocktail shaker with ice, and add gin, St-Germain, and lime juice; shake vigorously. Pour into an ice-filled rocks glass, and top off with club soda. Garnish, if desired.

3   STRAWBERRIES, HULLED

1½ TABLESPOONS (3 OUNCES) GIN

1   TABLESPOON (½ OUNCE) ST-GERMAIN LIQUEUR

1   TEASPOON (ABOUT ⅙ OUNCE) FRESH LIME JUICE

CLUB SODA

GARNISHES: STRAWBERRIES, LIME WEDGES, STRAWBERRY ICE CUBES

royal orchid

St-Germain's subtle elderflower flavor and light essence of lychee play nicely with the other spirits in this cocktail.

SERVES 1

Combine the first 5 ingredients in an ice-filled cocktail shaker, and shake vigorously. Strain into an ice-filled highball glass. Garnish, if desired

1½ TABLESPOONS (¾ OUNCE) ST-GERMAIN LIQUEUR

1   TABLESPOON (½ OUNCE) GIN

1   TABLESPOON (½ OUNCE) GOLD RUM

1   TABLESPOON (½ OUNCE) FRESH LIME JUICE

2   TABLESPOONS (1 OUNCE) GUAVA NECTAR OR PAPAYA JUICE

GARNISHES: LIME WEDGES, ORCHID BLOSSOMS

Bar Talk

SHAKING—

SHAKING IN AN ICE-FILLED COCKTAIL SHAKER FOR 12 SECONDS AERATES, BLENDS, AND OPTIMALLY CHILLS A COCKTAIL. USE CUBED ICE FOR MINIMAL DILUTION. STRAIN AND SERVE.

classic negroni

(COCKTAIL SHOWN)

3 TABLESPOONS (1½ OUNCES) CAMPARI

3 TABLESPOONS (1½ OUNCES) GIN

2 TABLESPOONS (1 OUNCE) SWEET VERMOUTH

GARNISHES: ORANGE ZEST TWIST, ORCHID BLOSSOM

Don't be fooled by its ruby hue—this drink is anything but sweet. The drink came to be at a bar near the banks of the Arno River in Florence, Italy, in 1919, when Count Negroni asked for gin instead of soda in his favorite cocktail, the Americano. The bartender obliged, mixing gin with scarlet Campari and sweet vermouth, and finished the cocktail with an orange rather than a lemon to signify it was a different drink. From 1860 until 2006, when the recipe changed, Campari got its red color from the bodies of red cochineal beetles.

SERVES 1

Combine the first 3 ingredients in an ice-filled glass, and stir well with a bar spoon. Strain into a coupe glass. Garnish, if desired.

cranberry negroni

1 CUP FRESH, OR FROZEN CRANBERRIES, THAWED

¼ CUP (2 OUNCES) SUGAR

2 CUPS (16 OUNCES) GIN

1 CUP (8 OUNCES) CAMPARI

1 CUP (8 OUNCES) SWEET VERMOUTH

8 DASHES OF BLOOD ORANGE BITTERS

8 THIN ORANGE ZEST STRIPS

Make sure you build in time to refrigerate the gin, cranberry, and sugar mixture at least overnight.

SERVES 4

1 Combine the cranberries and sugar in a small saucepan over medium. Cook, stirring occasionally (do not break berries), 7 minutes or until sugar dissolves. Transfer mixture to a large bowl, and let cool completely. Add the gin; cover and refrigerate 24 hours.

2 Pour the cranberry mixture through a fine wire-mesh strainer into a bowl. Reserve berries.

3 Combine ½ cup (4 ounces) strained gin, 2 tablespoons (2 ounces) Campari, 2 tablespoons (2 ounces) vermouth, and 4 dashes of bitters in an ice-filled cocktail shaker. Shake vigorously for 10 seconds, and strain into 2 rocks glasses. Garnish with orange zest and a few reserved berries. Repeat with remaining ingredients.

irish jig

(COCKTAIL SHOWN)

Shamrock green and as refreshing as springtime, gin and blue curaçao combine with midori (a melon liqueur) and ginger ale.

SERVES 1

Combine the first 4 ingredients in an ice-filled cocktail shaker, and shake vigorously. Strain into an ice-filled highball glass, and stir in ginger ale. Garnish, if desired.

2 TABLESPOONS (1 OUNCE) BOMBAY SAPPHIRE GIN

1½ TABLESPOONS (¾ OUNCE) MIDORI

1½ TEASPOONS (¼ OUNCE) BLUE CURAÇAO

JUICE OF ½ LIME

GINGER ALE

GARNISH: LIME WEDGE

floradora cocktail

Often made with raspberry syrup or liqueur and ginger beer, this version gets its fizz from neutral-flavored club soda, which lets the hit of fresh strawberry shine through.

SERVES 1

Combine the first 3 ingredients in an ice-filled cocktail shaker, and shake vigorously. Strain into an ice-filled Collins glass. Top off with a splash of Grenadine and club soda. Garnish, if desired.

6 TABLESPOONS (3 OUNCES) GIN

3 TABLESPOONS (1½ OUNCES) STRAWBERRY SYRUP (PAGE 19)

1 TABLESPOON (½ OUNCE) FRESH LIME JUICE

GRENADINE (PAGE 23)

CLUB SODA

GARNISHES: FRESH STRAWBERRIES, FRESH MINT SPRIG

killer bloody mary

(COCKTAIL PAGE 108)

BACON–BLOODY MARY RIM SALT
   (PAGE 32)

LIME WEDGE

1   TABLESPOON PREPARED
    HORSERADISH

DASH OF WORCESTERSHIRE SAUCE

DASH OF HOT SAUCE

PINCH OF CELERY SALT

PINCH OF CHOPPED FRESH DILL

PINCH OF FRESHLY CRACKED
    BLACK PEPPER

3   TABLESPOONS (1½ OUNCES)
    VODKA

⅔   CUP (ABOUT 5 OUNCES)
    CLAMATO TOMATO JUICE
    COCKTAIL

JUICE OF ½ LIME

GARNISHES: LIME WEDGE,
    PEPPERONCINO, PEPPADEWS,
    CELERY, PICKLES, OLIVES,
    OR OKRA

When it comes to Bloody Marys, the bolder the better. This "killer" recipe was adapted from Tara Guérard Soirée Event Planning and Design in Charleston, South Carolina—a city where Sunday brunch and booze are a longstanding tradition.

SERVES 1

1 Pour the Bacon–Bloody Mary Rim Salt on a shallow plate. Rub rim of a glass with lime wedge or damp finger, and twist rim of glass into salt.

2 Combine the next 6 ingredients in a highball glass. Fill glass with ice. Pour in the vodka, Clamato, and lime juice, and stir well. Garnish, if desired.

Bar Talk

CLAMATO—

A COMMERCIALLY AVAILABLE TOMATO-AND-CLAM JUICE BLEND THAT DELIVERS A DELICIOUSLY BRINY-UMAMI NOTE TO SEASIDE BLOODY MARYS.

An inviting cantina in the Mexican city of San Miguel de Allende opens up onto picturesque cobblestone streets.

basil tonic

(COCKTAIL SHOWN)

Vodka, fresh basil, simple syrup, and tonic water are all you need for this refreshingly easy cocktail. It's also a wonderful way to use basil leaves from an herb garden.

SERVES 1

Pour the Basil-Infused Vodka into an ice-filled highball glass. Stir in 1 tablespoon or desired amount of Lime-Basil Simple Syrup. Top off with tonic water. Garnish, if desired.

basil-infused vodka

Combine 2 cups (16 ounces) vodka and 1 cup lightly packed fresh basil leaves in a glass container. Crush basil gently with a muddler or wooden spoon to release flavor. Cover and set aside, out of direct sunlight, 2 days. Strain. Makes 2 cups

¼ CUP (2 OUNCES) BASIL-INFUSED VODKA

1 TABLESPOON (½ OUNCE) LIME-BASIL SIMPLE SYRUP OR SIMPLE SYRUP (PAGE 17)

⅓ TO ⅔ CUP (3 TO 5 OUNCES) TONIC WATER

GARNISHES: LIME SLICES, FRESH BASIL SPRIGS

christopher robin

Winnie the Pooh can't keep all the honey to himself. Sweet honey and bitter lemon take the spotlight in this refreshing drink, crafted by Nantucket's lovely restaurant and bar, Lola 41. For a spicy version, substitute our Jalapeño-Honey Syrup (page 18) for the honey.

SERVES 1

1 Combine a few drops of warm water and the honey, and stir until smooth.

2 Combine the vodka, lemon juice, and warm honey in an ice-filled cocktail shaker, and shake vigorously until thoroughly chilled, about 30 seconds. Strain into a martini glass. Garnish, if desired.

1½ TEASPOONS (¼ OUNCE) HONEY

5 TABLESPOONS (2½ OUNCES) BELVEDERE INTENSE VODKA

1½ TEASPOONS (¼ OUNCE) FRESH LEMON JUICE

GARNISH: LEMON WEDGE

MUSCAT, OMAN

Oman is home to an historic marketplace, the Mutrah Souq. Shoppers enter at a gate facing the Gulf of Oman.

omar sharif

Named after Lawrence of Arabia actor, Omar Sharif, this drink is sweet with a complex layering of the flavors and fragrance from citrus, pomegranate, and mint and a surprising kick of cinnamon that conjures Arabian nights with every sip.

⅓   CUP (2½ OUNCES) CITRUS VODKA

¼   CUP (2 OUNCES) POMEGRANATE LIQUEUR

¼   CUP (2 OUNCES) FRESH PINEAPPLE JUICE

1   TEASPOON (ABOUT ⅛ OUNCE) FRESH LEMON JUICE

GROUND CINNAMON

GARNISH: FRESH MINT SPRIG

SERVES 2

Combine the first 4 ingredients in an ice-filled cocktail shaker, and shake vigorously. Strain into 2 small ice-filled glasses. Sprinkle each with a pinch of cinnamon. Garnish, if desired.

This Palm Beach oasis, designed by Mario Nievera, suits the house's classic 1920s architecture.

palm beach martini

This shaken cocktail is a favorite from Table 26 in West Palm Beach.

SERVES 1

Combine the first 4 ingredients and a splash of Sour Mix in an ice-filled cocktail shaker, and shake vigorously for 20 seconds or until well chilled. Strain into a martini glass. Garnish, if desired.

5   TABLESPOONS (2½ OUNCES) TITO'S VODKA

1   TABLESPOON (½ OUNCE) ST-GERMAIN LIQUEUR

1   TABLESPOON (½ OUNCE) AGAVE NECTAR

6   TABLESPOONS (3 OUNCES) RUBY RED GRAPEFRUIT JUICE

SOUR MIX (PAGE 24)

GARNISH: GRAPEFRUIT WEDGE

classic dry martini

Do you take your martini shaken or stirred? James Bond's famous drink order has spurred much debate among bartenders.

SERVES 1

Pour the gin or vodka into an ice-filled cocktail shaker. Pour the dry vermouth in a martini glass, and swirl to coat. Pour the vermouth from the glass into the cocktail shaker. Stir with a bar spoon (or cover and shake vigorously), and pour (or strain) into prepared glass.

6   TABLESPOONS (3 OUNCES) GIN OR VODKA

1   TABLESPOON (½ OUNCE) DRY VERMOUTH

GARNISHES: LEMON ZEST TWIST, OLIVE, COCKTAIL ONION

Bar Talk

STIRRING—

BEST WHEN A SPIRIT IS COMBINED WITH MINIMAL MIXERS, THE DRINK IS BUILT IN AN ICE-FILLED SHAKER, GENTLY STIRRED WITH A BAR SPOON, AND STRAINED INTO THE GLASS.

Whiskey Primer

LONG BEFORE TENNESSEE claimed a stake on it, whiskey was rooted in Northern Europe. Stories claim that between the 11th and 13th centuries, Christian monks began distilling fermented barley in Scotland and Ireland. For these countries, making alcohol from grain was their only option: The cold, wet climates of the North were unsuited for growing grapes, so producing wine was impossible. Workers harvested grain, soaked it in hot water and yeast, distilled the liquid in copper pot stills, and aged the resulting whiskey in oak barrels.

By the turn of the 16th century, Scotland ruled whiskey production. Kings and laborers alike drank Scottish whiskey, known simply as "Scotch." The spirit's success was jeopardized in the 18th century, when England imposed strict taxes on unlicensed liquor production. To skirt the fees, distillers continued to make whiskey in secret at night to hide the telltale smoke. These illicit practices—lit only by the light of the moon—inspired the name of illegal brew: moonshine.

European whiskey-making methods, both legal and illegal, spread to the Americas, though each country's product has a distinct taste.

AMERICAN—Most American whiskeys are bourbons, made from corn. Tennessee whiskey, such as Jack Daniel's, is distinct because the whiskey is mellowed in maple charcoal after distillation.

CANADIAN—Called the "summer whiskey," Canadian whiskey is lighter than most whiskeys. It is made by mixing a light corn "base" with a rye "flavoring" whiskey.

IRISH—Most Irish whiskeys, like Jameson, are made from malted and unmalted barley. They are triple-distilled, resulting in a lighter taste than Scotch.

SCOTCH—Single malt scotch must be made from malted barley, in copper pot stills, and at a single distillery. Each Scotch develops a different local flavor, depending on its region.

1 SMALL FRESH MINT SPRIG

1 TABLESPOON (½ OUNCE) MINT
 SIMPLE SYRUP (PAGE 17)

2 TABLESPOONS (1 OUNCE)
 BOURBON

GARNISHES: POWDERED SUGAR,
 FRESH MINT SPRIG

mint julep

Although Mint Juleps are famous at Churchill Downs, these crisp drinks are just as delicious on a shoreline at sunset. The heavenly mix of bourbon, sugar, and fresh sprigs of mint makes for a refreshing sipper—no horses necessary.

SERVES 1

1 Muddle the mint sprig and syrup in the bottom and against the sides of a chilled julep cup to extract the oils.

2 Fill cup with crushed ice, and top off with bourbon. Garnish, if desired.

VARIATION:

cucumber mint julep: Muddle a thin ribbon of cucumber with mint sprig, and use equal parts Cucumber Simple Syrup (page 19) and Mint Simple Syrup (page 17).

A slower pace awaits alongside the May River in Palmetto Bluff, South Carolina.

manhattan

As the story goes, the Manhattan originated at New York City's Manhattan Club in the early 1870s when Winston Churchill's mother, Lady Randolph, threw a party for presidential candidate Samuel J. Tilden. The party's signature drink was famously dubbed the "Manhattan cocktail," after the name of the club.

SERVES 1

Combine the first 3 ingredients in a cocktail shaker, and shake vigorously. Pour into an ice-filled old-fashioned glass. Garnish, if desired.

6 TABLESPOONS (3 OUNCES) TENNESSEE WHISKEY

2 TEASPOONS (⅓ OUNCE) SWEET VERMOUTH

DASH OF ANGOSTURA BITTERS

GARNISHES: ORANGE ZEST TWIST, MARASCHINO CHERRIES

south of manhattan

This Southern spin on the whiskey classic, created by Jason Carlen at The Inn at Palmetto Bluff, South Carolina, relies on Kentucky bourbon tempered by fragrant almond liqueur and a sweet spike of maple syrup.

SERVES 1

Combine the first 4 ingredients in an ice-filled cocktail shaker, and shake vigorously. Strain into a cocktail glass. Garnish, if desired.

6 TABLESPOONS (3 OUNCES) KENTUCKY BOURBON

2 TO 4 TABLESPOONS (1 TO 2 OUNCES) AMARETTO

2 TABLESPOONS (1 OUNCE) PURE MAPLE SYRUP

1½ TEASPOONS (½ OUNCE) BLOOD ORANGE BITTERS

GARNISH: MARASCHINO CHERRY

indian summer cocktail

¼ CUP (2 OUNCES) BOURBON

1 TABLESPOON FRESH LEMON JUICE

1 TABLESPOON LEMONGRASS-CITRUS SHRUB SYRUP (PAGE 28)

1 TABLESPOON PEACH PRESERVES

GARNISHES: FRESH MINT SPRIGS, FRESH PEACH SLICES

Pure mouthwatering refreshment in a glass: Bourbon, citrus, an herbal shrub, and fruit combine in this heady cocktail.

SERVES 1

Combine the bourbon, lemon juice, Lemongrass-Citrus Shrub Syrup, and peach preserves in a cocktail shaker filled with ice. Cover and shake vigorously until chilled, about 15 seconds. Strain into a tumbler filled with ice. Garnish, if desired, and serve immediately.

The aptly named Soggy Dollar Bar on Jost Van Dyke in the British Virgin Islands serves up strong cocktails worth the swim to shore or wait for refreshment to come to you.

BRITISH VIRGIN ISLANDS

blood orange–bourbon coolers

(COCKTAIL SHOWN)

Blood oranges differ from their thick-skinned cousins, navel oranges, because they are less acidic in taste and have a richer, berry-like flavor. When pressed, blood oranges yield a tangy-sweet juice that pairs well with bourbon.

SERVES 4

Combine the first 4 ingredients in an ice-filled pitcher. Pour into ice-filled rocks glasses. Top off each with a dash of bitters, if desired. Garnish, if desired.

1   CUP (8 OUNCES) FRESH BLOOD ORANGE JUICE (ABOUT 4 ORANGES)

½   TO 1 CUP (4 TO 8 OUNCES) BOURBON

2   CUPS (16 OUNCES) REFRIGERATED LEMONADE

2   TABLESPOONS (1 OUNCE) REFRIGERATED POMEGRANATE JUICE

ANGOSTURA BITTERS (OPTIONAL)

GARNISH: BLOOD ORANGE SLICES

tangerine toddy

Another bourbon cocktail from The Inn at Palmetto Bluff in South Carolina is all the deliciousness of the classic hot toddy poured over ice. Substitute our Ginger-Honey Syrup (page 18) for bit of spiciness.

SERVES 1

Muddle the tangerine slice in a rocks glass, and add ice. Stir in the bourbon, lemon juice, and Honey Syrup.

honey syrup

Combine ¾ cup honey and ¼ cup hot water, stirring until blended; chill.

1   TANGERINE SLICE

3   TABLESPOONS (1½ OUNCES) BOURBON

1   TABLESPOON (½ OUNCE) FRESH LEMON JUICE

2   TABLESPOONS (1 OUNCE) HONEY SYRUP

Industrious English vacationers proposed building what is now the *Promenade des Anglais* around *Baie des Anges* (Bay of Angels), in Nice, France, in the early 1800s.

french cooler

(COCKTAIL SHOWN)

2 TABLESPOONS (1 OUNCE) YELLOW CHARTREUSE

1½ TABLESPOONS (¾ OUNCE) UNSWEETENED PINEAPPLE JUICE

1½ TABLESPOONS (¾ OUNCE) FRESH LIME JUICE

1 TABLESPOON (½ OUNCE) CURAÇAO

1 TABLESPOON (½ OUNCE) LILLET BLANC

1 TEASPOON (ABOUT ⅙ OUNCE) TOASTED ORGEAT SYRUP (PAGE 20)

GARNISHES: FRESH MINT SPRIG, ORANGE ZEST TWIST

First bottled in Bordeaux, France, in the 1870s, Kina Lillet (now labeled as Lillet Blanc) soon became an internationally known aperitif wine. In France, Lillet is served on ice with a slice of orange or lemon, but the subtly sweet and fruity wine shines in a mixed drink as well.

SERVES 1

Combine the first 6 ingredients in an ice-filled cocktail shaker, and shake vigorously. Strain into an ice-filled highball glass. Garnish, if desired.

french 75

2 TABLESPOONS (1 OUNCE) GIN OR LIGHT RUM

1 TABLESPOON (½ OUNCE) SIMPLE SYRUP (PAGE 17)

JUICE OF ½ LEMON

BRUT CHAMPAGNE

Crafted first in Paris in 1915, the French 75 was said to have the same punch as a French 75mm field gun. The drink certainly ups the ante of its close cousin, the Tom Collins, by using Champagne in the place of soda water.

SERVES 1

Combine the first 3 ingredients in an ice-filled cocktail shaker, and stir with a bar spoon. Strain into a champagne flute, and top off with Champagne.

pimm's cup

Pimm's No. 1 dates back to the 1840s, when a British fishmonger named James Pimm served the gin-and-herb aperitif liqueur to diners at his oyster bar. Today, Pimm's is famous across the Atlantic as well. In New Orleans, the Napoleon House bar serves a refreshing Pimm's Cup using Pimm's No. 1, lemonade, seltzer, and cucumber.

SERVES 1

Muddle the Cucumber Simple Syrup and 1 cucumber ribbon in the bottom and against the sides of a cocktail shaker. Add the Pimm's, gin, and lemon juice, and shake vigorously. Strain into an ice-filled highball glass. Top off with the club soda. Garnish, if desired.

1½ TABLESPOONS (¾ OUNCE) CUCUMBER SIMPLE SYRUP (PAGE 19)

2 LENGTHWISE-CUT CUCUMBER RIBBONS

3 TABLESPOONS (1½ OUNCES) PIMM'S NO. 1

1 TABLESPOON (½ OUNCE) GIN

2 TABLESPOONS (1 OUNCE) FRESH LEMON JUICE

CLUB SODA

GARNISH: FRESH MINT SPRIG, CUCUMBER RIBBON

absinthe drip

(COCKTAIL SHOWN)

Absinthe is a potent anise-flavored liquor made from the distillation of wormwood and botanicals. It can be clear (turning cloudy when the sugar water is added) or chartreuse. Part of the allure of the absinthe experience is in the meticulous making of the cocktail.

SERVES 1

1 Pour the absinthe into a chilled absinthe glass. Set a slotted spoon across the rim of the glass, and top with the sugar cube.

2 Secure an absinthe dripper (brouilleur) on the rim of the glass, and fill with ice and filtered ice water. Let water drip, very slowly, on the sugar cube. The sugar water will strain into the glass, turning the clear absinthe cloudy, and dissolving the sugar cube. When 4 to 6 ounces of water have filled the glass, remove the dripper and spoon. Stir gently before serving.

1 OUNCE ABSINTHE

1 SUGAR CUBE

FILTERED ICE WATER

grapefruit trinidad sour

(COCKTAIL TOP RIGHT, PAGE 135)

The Trinidad Sour was created by the bartender at Brooklyn's Clover Club; this cocktail is tropical in name and flavor alone. Ours adds a splash of grapefruit juice to the mix.

- 2 TABLESPOONS (1 OUNCE) GRAPEFRUIT BITTERS
- 2 TABLESPOONS (1 OUNCE) TOASTED ORGEAT SYRUP (PAGE 20)
- 1½ TABLESPOONS FRESH GRAPEFRUIT JUICE
- 1 TABLESPOON (½ OUNCE) RYE WHISKEY
- ½ TABLESPOON FRESH LEMON JUICE

GARNISH: GRAPEFRUIT ZEST TWIST

SERVES 1

1 Freeze a martini glass or coupe glass for 1 hour.

2 Combine the bitters, Orgeat Syrup, grapefruit juice, rye whiskey, and lemon juice in a cocktail shaker filled with ice. Cover and shake vigorously until chilled, about 30 seconds. Strain into frozen glass. Garnish, if desired.

amaretto sour

(COCKTAIL BOTTOM RIGHT, PAGE 134)

Amaretto is Italian for "a little bitter," an apt description of the almond liqueur. The beauty of amaretto is its diversity—it enhances the flavors of tiramisú, flavors savory meat dishes, and mingles with lemon and salt in a sweet-and-sour cocktail.

CITRUS RIM SALT (PAGE 32)

LEMON WEDGE

- ¼ CUP (2 OUNCES) AMARETTO
- 2 TABLESPOONS (1 OUNCE) FRESH LEMON JUICE

GARNISH: MARASCHINO CHERRY

SERVES 1

1 Pour the salt on a shallow plate. Rub rim of a stemless wineglass with lemon wedge, and dip rim of glass in salt, twisting to coat. Drop the lemon wedge in the glass and fill with ice.

2 Combine the amaretto and lemon juice in a cocktail shaker, and shake vigorously. Pour into prepared glass. Garnish, if desired.

brandy sour

(COCKTAIL BOTTOM RIGHT, PAGE 135)

When Egyptian King Farouk vacationed in the Mediterranean region of Cyprus in the 1930s, he had a penchant for Western cocktails. His hosts whipped up a Brandy Sour, and the cocktail was so popular that it became the national drink of Cyprus.

SERVES 1

Combine the first 3 ingredients in an ice-filled cocktail shaker, and shake vigorously. Strain into an ice-filled rocks glass. Top off with the lemonade or club soda. Garnish, if desired.

6   TABLESPOONS (3 OUNCES) BRANDY OR COGNAC

3   TABLESPOONS (1½ OUNCES) SOUR MIX (PAGE 24)

2   DROPS OF ANGOSTURA BITTERS

LEMONADE OR CLUB SODA

GARNISHES: LEMON WEDGE, MARASCHINO CHERRY

midori sour

(COCKTAIL TOP LEFT, PAGE 134)

Midori is a candy-sweet musk-melon liqueur made in Japan exclusively until the late 80s. It gets its name from the Japanese word for melon.

SERVES 1

Fill a cocktail shaker with the ice. Add the Midori and next 3 ingredients, and shake vigorously. Strain the mixture into a glass. Garnish, if desired.

1   CUP ICE CUBES

2   TABLESPOONS (¼ OUNCE) MIDORI

1   TABLESPOON (½ OUNCE) FRESH LIME JUICE

1   TABLESPOON (½ OUNCE) WATER

2   TABLESPOONS (1 OUNCE) SUPERFINE SUGAR

GARNISH: MELON BALLS

Egg Whites in Cocktails

FOAM GETS A BAD RAP. In the ocean, it smudges the crispness of the waves; atop a pint of beer, it traps the amber liquid underneath. But for some drinks, foam isn't a distraction, but a taste enhancer. Enter: egg whites in cocktails.

Egg whites are unique because they are practically tasteless, but their addition to cocktails like the Pisco Sour and Silver Fizz can boost the drinks from average to exquisite. This is due to the proteins in egg whites, which help bind other cocktail ingredients together, melding them into a rich, creamy sip. So when it comes to egg whites in cocktails, it's all about the textural element that they provide. When whipped or shaken, egg white proteins stretch out, creating a delicate foam cap that floats like a raft atop the cocktail. Shaking also emulsifies the egg whites with the other liquid ingredients, resulting in a velvety mouthfeel that gives unexpected richness to drinks. Spirits help to keep the whipped whites slightly liquid—so there's no need to worry about the foam cap stiffening like a meringue.

For best results, combine egg whites in a shaker with the other ingredients, and then give it a dry shake (without ice)—this prevents the cocktail from being too watery, and lets the egg whites form a frothy foam without obstruction. Combining them with the ice won't ruin the experience, though, to be sure. Don't be afraid of white caps in your drink. Embrace every foamy, frothy, sublime sip.

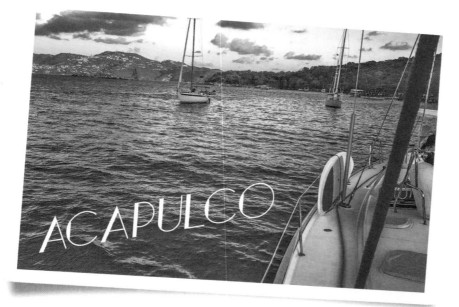
ACAPULCO

A vacation mecca for the Hollywood jet set in the 50s and 60s, Acapulco remains Mexico's most popular tourist resort.

acapulco

¼ CUP (2 OUNCES) WHITE RUM

2 TABLESPOONS MINT SIMPLE SYRUP OR SIMPLE SYRUP (PAGE 17)

2 TABLESPOONS FRESH LIME JUICE

1½ TABLESPOONS (¾ OUNCE) TRIPLE SEC

1 LARGE PASTEURIZED EGG WHITE

1 FRESH MINT SPRIG, PLUS 1 FOR GARNISH

This minty refresher has the thick texture of a frozen drink thanks to the egg white, but with much less effort.

SERVES 1

Combine the rum, Mint Simple Syrup, lime juice, Triple Sec, egg white, and 1 mint sprig in a cocktail shaker; fill with ice. Cover with lid, and shake vigorously 45 seconds. Strain into a chilled rocks glass filled with crushed ice. Garnish with a mint sprig, if desired.

calm voyage

The name of this cocktail belies its frothy texture after a whirl in the blender. However, the liquid begins to separate from the foam as the drink is enjoyed.

SERVES 1

1 Place the passion fruit nectar and sugar in a small saucepan over medium-high, and cook, stirring constantly, until sugar is dissolved, 1 to 2 minutes. Remove from heat, and cool slightly. Chill mixture at least 30 minutes.

2 Process the rum, Chartreuse, lemon juice, egg white, and passion fruit mixture in a blender until thickened and smooth, about 20 seconds. Pour into a chilled champagne flute.

3 TABLESPOONS PASSION FRUIT NECTAR

1 TABLESPOON GRANULATED SUGAR

3 TABLESPOONS (1½ OUNCES) WHITE RUM

1 TABLESPOON (½ OUNCE) GREEN CHARTRUESE

1 TABLESPOON FRESH LEMON JUICE

1 LARGE PASTEURIZED EGG WHITE

boxcar

3 TABLESPOONS (1½ OUNCES) GIN

1 TABLESPOON (½ OUNCE) TRIPLE
   SEC

1 TABLESPOON FRESH LEMON
   JUICE

2 TEASPOONS GRENADINE
   (PAGE 23)

1 LARGE PASTEURIZED EGG
   WHITE

GARNISH: LEMON ZEST TWIST

This scarlet tipple gets it rosy hue from Grenadine, which also lends sweetness to round out the citrus notes.

SERVES 1

Combine the gin, Triple Sec, lemon juice, Grenadine, and egg white in a cocktail shaker; fill with ice. Cover with lid, and shake vigorously 45 seconds. Strain into a chilled martini glass. Garnish, if desired.

Bar Talk

TWIST—
A CURLED STRIP OF CITRUS
ZEST IS MORE THAN A PRETTY
FLOURISH TWISTED ABOVE
THE GLASS: THE RIND'S
AROMATIC OILS IMPART
FLAVOR AND A FRAGRANT
NOTE TO COCKTAILS.

silver fizz

This bubbly, boozy cocktail with its raft of foam is mellow and subtly flavored by lemon and gin's juniper bite.

SERVES 1

Combine the gin, Simple Syrup, lemon juice, and egg white in a cocktail shaker. Fill with ice; cover with lid, and shake vigorously 45 seconds. Strain into a chilled highball glass, and top with seltzer and ice. Stir gently. Garnish, if desired.

¼ CUP (2 OUNCES) GIN

2 TABLESPOONS SIMPLE SYRUP (PAGE 17)

2 TABLESPOONS FRESH LEMON JUICE

1 LARGE PASTEURIZED EGG WHITE

½ CUP (4 OUNCES) SELTZER WATER

GARNISH: LEMON ZEST TWIST

Bar Talk

FIZZ—

IN THE FAMILY OF SOUR COCKTAILS THAT INCORPORATE EGG WHITES INTO THE MIX, A CLASSIC FIZZ MIXES IN CITRUS AND SELTZER, TOO, FOR A BRIGHT AND BUBBLY COCKTAIL.

Caballitos de totora, native fishing boats made out of reeds, dry in the sun on the beach at Pimentel in Chiclayo, Peru.

pisco sour

(COCKTAIL SHOWN)

3 TABLESPOONS (1½ OUNCES) PISCO

1½ TABLESPOONS (¾ OUNCE) SIMPLE SYRUP (PAGE 17)

1 TABLESPOON (½ OUNCE) FRESH LIME JUICE OR KEY LIME JUICE

1 LARGE PASTEURIZED EGG WHITE

2 DROPS OF ANGOSTURA BITTERS

GARNISH: LIME SLICE

Pisco hails from the coastal cradle of Pisco on the border of Peru and Chile. Legends say that when the Spanish conquistadors invaded Peru in the 16th century, they planted vast vineyards in the arid country, and then distilled the wine the grapes produced into an amber-colored brandy. Pisco is traditionally taken on the rocks, but is great in cocktails, too.

SERVES 1

Combine the first 4 ingredients in an ice-filled cocktail shaker, and shake vigorously. Strain into a highball glass. Add a few drops of the bitters. Stir with a bar spoon or swizzle stick. Garnish, if desired.

pisco sunset

6 TABLESPOONS (3 OUNCES) PISCO

¼ CUP (2 OUNCES) CAMPARI

3 TABLESPOONS (1½ OUNCES) FRESH ORANGE JUICE

3 TABLESPOONS (1½ OUNCES) PEAR NECTAR

GARNISH: ORANGE ZEST TWIST

Consider this the pisco version of a Tequila Sunrise, swapping out Grenadine for Campari and rounding out the citrus with a splash of pear nectar to create a new happy hour favorite.

SERVES 1

Combine the first 4 ingredients in an ice-filled cocktail shaker, and shake vigorously. Strain into a glass. Garnish, if desired.

bushwacker

The origin of this recipe is hotly contested. The Sandshaker Bar in Pensacola, Florida, claims its creation as does the Sapphire Pub in St. Thomas, U.S. Virgin Islands. We're just thankful it exists. It's a cooling respite on a hot, summer day or a decadent dinner finale.

SERVES 4

Combine first 7 ingredients in a blender, cover with lid, process until finely chopped. Add ice cream, and process until smooth. Pour into parfait glasses. Garnish, if desired.

3   CUPS CRUSHED ICE

½   CUP (4 OUNCES) CREAM OF COCONUT

¼   CUP (2 OUNCES) COFFEE LIQUEUR, CHILLED

¼   CUP (2 OUNCES) IRISH CREAM LIQUEUR, CHILLED

¼   CUP (2 OUNCES) DARK CRÈME DE CACAO LIQUEUR, CHILLED

¼   CUP (2 OUNCES) BLACK OR DARK RUM, CHILLED

2   TABLESPOONS (1 OUNCE) CHOCOLATE SAUCE OR SYRUP

4   CUPS VANILLA ICE CREAM

GARNISHES: WHIPPED CREAM, MARASCHINO CHERRIES

This 32-square-mile paradise was the inspiring home of French Impressionist painter Camille Pissaro.

ST. THOMAS

coconut eggnog

Coconut rum, coconut milk, and shaved coconut pieces on top make this a true coconut lover's paradise.

SERVES 6

- 1½ CUPS (12 OUNCES) HEAVY CREAM
- 2 LARGE EGGS, BEATEN
- 1 (13.5-OUNCE) CAN COCONUT MILK
- 1 (14-OUNCE) CAN SWEETENED CONDENSED MILK
- 1 CUP (8 OUNCES) COCONUT RUM
- 1 TABLESPOON (½ OUNCE) VANILLA EXTRACT
- ½ TO 1 TEASPOON GROUND CINNAMON
- ¼ TO ½ TEASPOON GROUND CLOVES
- GARNISHES: SHAVED COCONUT, GROUND CINNAMON, CINNAMON STICKS

1 Pour water to a depth of 1 inch into bottom of a double boiler over medium; bring to a boil. Reduce heat, and simmer; place cream and eggs in top of double boiler over simmering water. Cook, stirring constantly, 4 minutes or until mixture thickens and reaches 160°F. Remove from heat, and transfer to a large bowl.

2 Stir in coconut milk and next 5 ingredients. Cover and chill 3 hours. Garnish, if desired.

Bar Talk

NOG—

A REFERENCE TO A BREWED ALE SERVED IN A NOGGIN, OR WOODEN MUG, OR A MILK PUNCH OF CREAM, EGGS, AND A DISTILLED SPIRIT SUCH AS BOURBON, BRANDY, OR RUM.

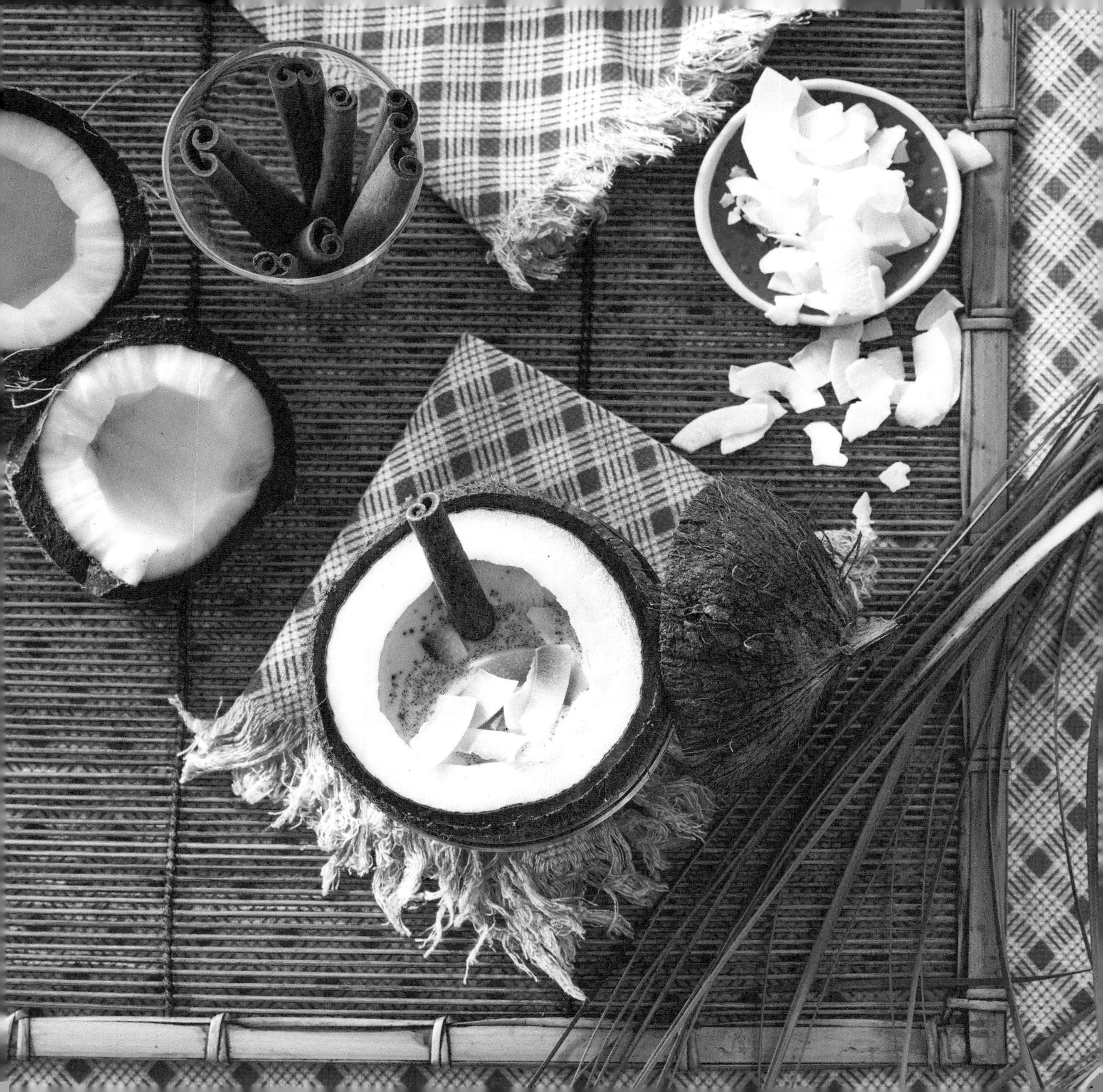

frosty cappuccino

No ice trays? Pour the coffee into 2½ dozen small paper cups, place on a baking pan, and then freeze.

SERVES 6

Freeze the coffee in ice cube trays. Combine frozen coffee and remaining ingredients in a blender, cover with lid, and process until smooth. Serve in rocks glasses or stemless wineglasses.

3½ CUPS (28 OUNCES) STRONG BREWED COFFEE

1 CUP (8 OUNCES) CHOCOLATE MILK

¼ TEASPOON GROUND CINNAMON

⅓ CUP (3 OUNCES) BOURBON

2 CUPS COFFEE ICE CREAM

KAUAI, HAWAII

Hawaii is the only state in the United States able to grow coffee on farms like the one seen in this aerial photo.

sea island milk punch

2 CUPS (16 OUNCES) HEAVY
WHIPPING CREAM

2 CUPS (16 OUNCES) WHOLE MILK

1 CUP (8 OUNCES) WOODFORD
RESERVE BOURBON

¾ CUP (2½ OUNCES) SIFTED
POWDERED SUGAR

½ VANILLA BEAN, SPLIT

GRATED FRESH NUTMEG

*For holiday happy hour, try this decadent milk punch from
Georgia's luxury Sea Island Resort.*

SERVES 4

1 Combine the first 4 ingredients in a metal bowl placed in a
bowl of ice and water. Scrape seeds from vanilla bean into cream
mixture; discard pod. Whisk until frothy.

2 Pour into an 8-cup pitcher, and freeze 30 to 60 minutes,
stirring occasionally.

3 Pour into 4 rocks glasses or old-fashioned glasses, and
sprinkle with the grated nutmeg.

Bar Talk

PUNCH—
FROM THE SANSKRIT "PAÑC"
OR "FIVE," CLASSIC PUNCH
WAS A MIX OF FIVE INGREDIENTS:
ALCOHOL, SUGAR, WATER,
LEMON, TEA OR SPICES.

Forming the Avenue of the Oaks, these 160-year-old live oak trees make an impressive entrance to Sea Island Golf Club.

creamy milk punch

Horchata liqueur is a creamy mix of rum and spices that, when blended with whole milk, bourbon, and lime juice (surprise!), creates a delicious, booze-infused milk punch.

SERVES 1

Combine the first 5 ingredients in an ice-filled cocktail shaker, and shake vigorously until thoroughly chilled, about 30 seconds. Strain into a mug. Garnish, if desired.

¼ CUP (2 OUNCES) WHOLE MILK

3 TABLESPOONS (1½ OUNCES) HORCHATA LIQUEUR (SUCH AS RUMCHATA)

1½ TABLESPOONS (¾ OUNCE) BOURBON

1 TABLESPOON (½ OUNCE) AMARETTO

¼ TEASPOON FRESH LIME JUICE

GARNISH: GRATED FRESH NUTMEG

Indonesia's Banda Islands figured prominently during the 17th century spice trade thanks to the nutmeg trees that once grew almost exclusively on their shores.

brandy milk punch

(COCKTAIL ON LEFT)

Old-fashioned and filling, this punch is based on a mix of dairy milks.

SERVES 8

2   CUPS (16 OUNCES) HALF-AND-HALF

2   CUPS (16 OUNCES) WHOLE MILK

1   TO 1⅓ CUPS (8 TO 12 OUNCES) BRANDY

½   CUP (4 OUNCES) SIMPLE SYRUP (PAGE 17)

1   TEASPOON (ABOUT ⅛ OUNCE) VANILLA EXTRACT

2   CUPS CRUSHED ICE

GROUND NUTMEG

Whisk together all the ingredients except nutmeg in a large bowl. Pour through a wire-mesh strainer into chilled brandy snifters. Sprinkle with the nutmeg.

creamy winter nog

(COCKTAIL ON RIGHT)

Melted ice cream and a shot of coffee liqueur combine in a stick-to-your-ribs concoction that will take you to nog nirvana.

SERVES 6 TO 8

1   QUART VANILLA ICE CREAM, SOFTENED

½   TO ¾ CUP (4 TO 6 OUNCES) BRANDY

6   TABLESPOONS (3 OUNCES) COFFEE LIQUEUR

¼   TEASPOON GROUND NUTMEG

GARNISH: WHIPPED CREAM

Combine the first 3 ingredients in a large bowl, and stir until smooth. Pour into glass mugs or Irish coffee cups, and sprinkle with nutmeg. Garnish, if desired. Serve immediately.

A cliff-hugging road leads to the scenic Coumeenoole Beach on the Dingle Peninsula in County Kerry, Ireland.

irish flag

Celebrate the Emerald Isle with this layered cocktail in the colors of the Irish flag.

SERVES 1

Pour the crème de menthe into a cordial glass. Take a teaspoon and touch the edge of the spoon to the inside of the glass, the round side up just at the surface of the crème de menthe layer. Gently pour the Irish cream onto the rounded spoon back forming a white layer above the green layer. Repeat the process with the brandy for a layer of orange to create a finished drink with bands of green, white, and orange.

2 TABLESPOONS (1 OUNCE) GREEN CRÈME DE MENTHE

2 TABLESPOONS (1 OUNCE) IRISH CREAM LIQUEUR (SUCH AS BAILEYS)

2 TABLESPOONS (1 OUNCE) BRANDY

the nutty irishman

Celebrate St. Paddy's Day with this new signature cocktail—The Nutty Irishman—from Dromoland Castle, County Clare, Ireland. Two tasty liqueurs make up this popular after-dinner drink.

SERVES 1

Fill a brandy snifter half full with ice. Top with the Irish cream and Frangelico, and stir.

2 TABLESPOONS (1 OUNCE) IRISH CREAM LIQUEUR (SUCH AS BAILEYS)

2 TABLESPOONS (1 OUNCE) FRANGELICO

frozen white chocolate

(COCKTAIL ON RIGHT)

¼ CUP (2 OUNCES) WHITE
    CHOCOLATE LIQUEUR

¼ CUP (2 OUNCES) IRISH CREAM
    LIQUEUR (SUCH AS BAILEYS)

2 TABLESPOONS (1 OUNCE)
   CLEAR CRÈME DE CACAO

3 CUPS VANILLA ICE CREAM

GARNISH: GRATED FRESH NUTMEG

Drink your dessert with this decadent milkshake-for-adults. It features white chocolate liqueur, Irish cream, crème de cacao, and plenty of vanilla ice cream.

SERVES 2 TO 3

Combine the first 4 ingredients in a blender, cover with lid, and process until smooth. Pour into 2 parfait glasses or 3 rocks glasses. Serve with straws and spoons. Garnish, if desired.

grasshopper

(COCKTAIL ON LEFT)

2 TABLESPOONS (1 OUNCE) WHITE
   CRÈME DE MENTHE

2 TABLESPOONS (1 OUNCE) WHITE
   CRÈME DE CACAO

2 TABLESPOONS (1 OUNCE)
   WHIPPING CREAM

GARNISH: FRESH MINT SPRIG

This three-ingredient cocktail is a festive twist on the standard bar offering. A creamy, minty after-dinner drink, it's best enjoyed with a sweet dessert.

SERVES 1

Combine the first 3 ingredients in a cocktail shaker, and shake vigorously. Strain into a glass. Garnish, if desired.

spiked almond milk (horchata)

Horchata is a Latin nut-and-seed milk infused with warm spices like cinnamon. Some cultures include rice to thicken and others add dairy milk to the blend. Latin countries have been soaking and grinding rice and nuts into milk for centuries, and then adding spices and flavorings to create complex flavors. Horchata is a standard offering at aguas frescas stands. To make a horchata cocktail, add amaretto to up the almond flavor, horchata liqueur, or dark rum.

SERVES 6

1 Combine 3 cups of the water and next 6 ingredients in a large bowl. Cover and chill 8 hours or overnight until solids are soft. Strain mixture through a fine wire-mesh strainer, reserving solids. Discard liquid.

2 Place solids, remaining 1 cup water, almond milk, and amaretto in a blender; process 2 minutes. Strain through a fine wire-mesh strainer into a pitcher, and discard solids. Add the Simple Syrup, extracts, and salt to milk mixture, stirring to combine. Serve over ice.

4   CUPS WATER

¾   CUP LONG-GRAIN RICE

½   CUP SLIVERED ALMONDS

1   TABLESPOON FINELY GRATED ORANGE ZEST

3   CINNAMON STICKS, BROKEN IN PIECES

3   WHOLE ALLSPICE

3   WHOLE CLOVES

1½ CUPS (12 OUNCES) UNSWEETENED ALMOND MILK

1½ CUPS (12 OUNCES) AMARETTO, HORCHATA LIQUEUR, OR DARK RUM

¼   CUP (2 OUNCES) SIMPLE SYRUP (PAGE 17)

1   TEASPOON (ABOUT ⅛ OUNCE) VANILLA EXTRACT

¼   TEASPOON ALMOND EXTRACT

DASH OF SALT

Cocktails as Curatives

WHEN "COCKTAILS" WERE FIRST introduced in print in 1803, they were just what the doctor ordered—literally. Composed simply of spirits, sugar, and bitters, cocktails were considered curatives for a range of maladies, from acute stomachaches to bouts of depression.

Before medicinal advances in the 1900s, spirits mystified doctors. They believed alcohol to be both a stimulant and depressant, able to both numb excruciating pain and enhance joy. Because of their high caloric density, spirits were even thought to be a worthy nutritional supplement, especially for ill patients who couldn't stomach food. In serious cases, according to some reports, doctors would even inject shots of brandy into patients' veins.

Alcohol aside, the key ingredient to the "curative" cocktail of the early 1900s was bitters. Made with a combination of herbs and botanicals, bitters were akin to ancient healing remedies, and they were thought to restore the body's wellness. Angostura bitters, invented in Venezuela in 1824, were famous for curing sailors' seasickness. Orange bitters, made from orange rinds and spices, supposedly had rejuvenating qualities.

Depending on the combination of bitters and alcohol, curative cocktails could be categorized as "stimulants," "painkillers," or "stress relievers." Whether the drinks really cured bodily sickness still remains a mystery, but they certainly boost the human spirit.

2 TABLESPOONS (1 OUNCE) TOFFEE SAUCE

3 TABLESPOONS (1½ OUNCES) MT. GAY BLACK BARREL RUM

GARNISH: CINNAMON STICK

hot buttered rum

Crafted by the Presidio Social Club in San Francisco, this decadent, warming drink can stave off the chill of the bay.

SERVES 1

Combine the Toffee Sauce and rum in an 8-ounce glass. Fill with hot water, and stir. Garnish, if desired.

toffee sauce

7 OUNCES (¾ CUP PLUS 2 TABLESPOONS) SALTED BUTTER

¾ CUP (ABOUT 5⅔ OUNCES) PACKED BROWN SUGAR

¼ TEASPOON GRATED FRESH NUTMEG

1½ TEASPOONS GROUND CINNAMON

¼ TEASPOON GROUND CLOVES

¾ CUP (6 OUNCES) HEAVY CREAM

Bring the first 5 ingredients to a boil in a medium saucepan over medium. Boil, stirring constantly, 1 minute. Stir in the cream; return to a boil. Remove from heat, and strain through a fine wire-mesh strainer. Makes 1½ cups

tom and jerry

The batter used in this Old World eggnog cocktail is delicious atop an array of hot drinks like cocoa, chai, Irish coffee, and Hot Buttered Rum (page 176).

SERVES 2

1 Make the batter: Beat the egg whites and cream of tartar in a small mixing bowl until soft peaks form. In a separate bowl, beat the egg yolks and rum. Gradually add the sugar and spices to the yolks, whisking until combined. Gently fold the egg whites into the yolks with a flexible spatula.

2 Make the cocktail: Spoon the batter into a large liquid measuring cup. Gently stir in the rum, brandy, and hot milk until just incorporated. Divide cocktail evenly among 2 large, warmed mugs. Garnish, if desired.

BATTER:

4 LARGE EGGS, SEPARATED

⅛ TEASPOON CREAM OF TARTAR

1 TABLESPOON (½ OUNCE) DARK RUM

½ CUP SUPERFINE SUGAR

PINCH OF GROUND CINNAMON

PINCH OF GRATED FRESH NUTMEG

PINCH OF GROUND ALLSPICE

SCANT PINCH OF GROUND CLOVES

COCKTAIL:

½ CUP BATTER

2 TABLESPOONS (1 OUNCE) DARK RUM

2 TABLESPOONS (1 OUNCE) BRANDY

½ CUP HOT WHOLE MILK

GARNISHES: GROUND CINNAMON, CINNAMON STICKS (OPTIONAL)

Bar Talk

COCKTAIL BATTER—

RICHER THAN THE USUAL EGG WHITES THAT LEND BODY TO DRINKS, A BATTER IS MADE FROM BEATEN EGG WHITES FOLDED INTO YOLKS WITH SUGAR, LIQUOR, AND SPICES.

jamaican black stripe

¾ CUP WATER

1 TABLESPOON MOLASSES

1 (3-INCH) LEMON ZEST STRIP

¼ CUP (2 OUNCES) DARK RUM

GARNISH: LEMON WEDGE

Served hot or cold with multiple variations, this rich drink is called Black Strap (perhaps a nod to the molasses), Bombo, or Black Stripe depending on what region of the world is serving it up.

SERVES 1

Bring the water to a boil in a small saucepan over high. Remove from heat; stir in molasses and lemon zest strip. Cover and steep 8 minutes. Discard the lemon zest strip; stir rum into molasses liquid. Pour into a heat-safe glass or mug. Garnish, if desired.

Not far from Ocho Rios, the impressive Dunn's River Falls are terraced like giant stairs more than 600 feet and empty into the Caribbean Sea.

OCHO RIOS, JAMAICA

moroccan-mint tea toddy

(COCKTAIL BOTTOM LEFT, PAGE 182)

A "toddy" might conjure Grandma's bedtime tipple, but warm cocktails develop complex flavors in a way no chilled cocktail can.

SERVES 1

- ¾ CUP BOILING WATER
- 1 REGULAR-SIZE MOROCCAN MINT TEA BAG
- 2 TABLESPOONS (1 OUNCE) BOURBON
- 1 TABLESPOON GINGER-HONEY SYRUP (PAGE 18) OR HONEY

Place the boiling water in a heat-safe glass or mug; add tea bag, and let steep 5 minutes. Discard tea bag. Stir in the bourbon and Ginger-Honey Syrup.

chai hot toddy

(COCKTAIL BOTTOM RIGHT, PAGE 183)

Spices meet warm tea and brandy in a restorative cocktail that's as ideal after a blustery day at the beach as it is after skiing.

SERVES 1

- 1 CUP WATER
- 1 REGULAR-SIZE BLACK TEA BAG
- 1 (2-INCH) CINNAMON STICK
- 2 WHOLE CLOVES
- 2 CARDAMOM PODS
- 1 STAR ANISE POD
- 1 (3-INCH) ORANGE ZEST STRIP
- 3 TABLESPOONS (1½ OUNCES) BRANDY

Bring the water to a boil in a small saucepan over high. Remove pan from heat; add tea bag and next 5 ingredients. Steep 10 minutes; remove and discard tea bag. Steep in pan 20 minutes. Pour through a wire-mesh strainer into a bowl; discard spices and orange strip. Pour liquid into saucepan, and heat until warm. Pour into a heat-safe glass or mug, and stir in brandy.

irish coffee

(COCKTAIL TOP LEFT, PAGE 182)

Bold coffee and Irish whiskey are tempered with sweet cream and brown sugar, making a mug you'll want to wrap your fingers around. Beat the cream ever so slightly, for a thickened layer to float atop the coffee.

SERVES 1

Fill an Irish coffee mug with the boiling water to warm; pour out water. Add the sugar to the bottom of the mug and top with whiskey. Pour in the coffee. Pour the cream slowly over the back of a spoon, inverted over the mug. Do not stir. (The drink is meant to be sipped through the layer of cream.)

BOILING WATER

2 TO 3 TEASPOONS DARK BROWN SUGAR

¼ CUP (2 OUNCES) IRISH WHISKEY

¾ CUP (6 OUNCES) HOT BREWED COFFEE

2 TABLESPOONS (1 OUNCE) HEAVY CREAM, WHIPPED

boozy almond-honey hot chocolate

(COCKTAIL TOP RIGHT, PAGE 183)

Hot cocoa combines with amaretto in this decadent treat.

SERVES 4

1 Bring the milk, 1 cup of the heavy cream, and vanilla bean to a simmer in a small saucepan over medium. Remove from heat. Whisk in amaretto, honey, chocolate, and salt. Keep warm.

2 Whisk remaining heavy cream in a chilled bowl until soft peaks form. Serve topped with whipped cream and the almonds.

3 CUPS (24 OUNCES) WHOLE MILK

1½ CUPS (12 OUNCES) HEAVY CREAM

1 VANILLA BEAN, SPLIT

¾ CUP (6 OUNCES) AMARETTO

¼ CUP (2 OUNCES) HONEY

3 OUNCES CHOPPED MILK CHOCOLATE

⅛ TEASPOON KOSHER SALT

TOASTED SLICED ALMONDS

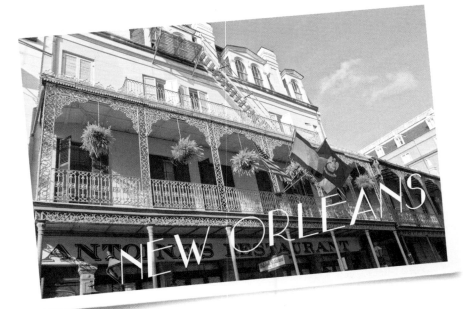

Jules Alciatore, the son of the owner of Antoine's Restaurant, created this hot toddy as a means of hiding alcohol during Prohibition.

café brûlot diabolique

1 ORANGE

1 LEMON

1 (1-OUNCE) BOTTLE CINNAMON STICKS

2 TABLESPOONS (1 OUNCE) WHOLE CLOVES

3 TABLESPOONS SUGAR

⅔ CUP (ABOUT 6 OUNCES) GRAND MARNIER OR OTHER ORANGE LIQUEUR

⅔ CUP (ABOUT 6 OUNCES) BRANDY

6 CUPS (40 OUNCES) HOT BREWED COFFEE

GARNISH: CITRUS WEDGES

In New Orleans, Café Brûlot (devilishly burned coffee) is more than a drink order—it's an event. It was born at Antoine's Restaurant, where waiters pour the coffee-brandy mixture into a silver bowl and light the liquid on fire. Holding orange zest twists just above the bowl, the waiter pours the flaming drink down the peel, creating a striking orange and blue ribbon of fire as the alcohol burns off.

SERVES 6

1 Peel the orange and the lemon, each in one long strip. Squeeze the orange, reserving 2 tablespoons juice. Reserve peeled lemon for another use.

2 Combine the orange peel, lemon peel, and next 5 ingredients in a nonaluminum saucepan. Cook over medium, stirring occasionally, 3 minutes or until thoroughly heated. Stir in reserved orange juice.

3 Pour the mixture through a wire-mesh strainer into the coffee; discard solids. Stir and serve immediately. Garnish, if desired.

From its 93-foot vantage point as the tallest lighthouse on the Oregon Coast, the Yaquina Head Light stands above the only wheelchair-accessible tide pools in the country.

cupola house wassail

1 GALLON APPLE CIDER

2 (12-OUNCE) CANS FROZEN LEMONADE CONCENTRATE, THAWED

3 (3-INCH) CINNAMON STICKS

1 TABLESPOON GROUND CLOVES

½ TEASPOON GROUND ALLSPICE

4 DRIED APPLE RINGS

1 ORANGE, THINLY SLICED

1 LEMON, THINLY SLICED

4 CUPS (32 OUNCES) WHITE WINE

The Cupola House, a historic home and gardens on Edenton Bay in North Carolina, serves this warm and soothing wassail every year during its holiday celebration.

SERVES 20

1 Combine the first 5 ingredients in a large nonaluminum pan. Bring to a boil, reduce heat, and simmer 15 minutes.

2 Place the dried apple rings, orange slices, and lemon slices in the bottom of a punch bowl. Add the white wine. Stir in the warm cider mixture.

Bar Talk

WASSAIL—

A HOT MULLED (SPICED) HARD APPLE CIDER THAT GOT ITS NAME FROM THE MEDIEVAL GREETING "WAES HAIL" (BE HEALTHY), WASSAIL HAS BECOME A REFERENCE TO ANY HOT MULLED PUNCH.

mulled cider and wine

(COCKTAIL SHOWN)

This warm drink calls for a quick simmer with juices and spices, and then an easy addition of red wine just before serving.

SERVES 10 TO 12

Combine the first 9 ingredients in a large nonaluminum saucepan over medium heat. Simmer 30 minutes. Pour in the wine, and stir until thoroughly heated. Serve warm.

4 CUPS (32 OUNCES) APPLE CIDER

4 CUPS (32 OUNCES) ORANGE-PINEAPPLE JUICE

½ CUP (3½ OUNCES) SUGAR

6 CINNAMON STICKS

1 TEASPOON WHOLE ALLSPICE

1 TEASPOON WHOLE CLOVES

1 (2-INCH) PIECE FRESH GINGER, PEELED AND SLICED

1 LEMON, SLICED

1 ORANGE, SLICED

4 CUPS (32 OUNCES) RED WINE

smoking bishop

Several Victorian-era hot toddy punches named for High-Church clerics are known as "ecclesiastics." The Pope, Archbishop, and Cardinal cocktails all incorporate a particular wine varietal and are served punch-bowl style for communal enjoyment. The Bishop is the port-based warm punch that Dickens refers to in A Christmas Carol.

SERVES 10 TO 12

1 Preheat the oven to 400°F. Place a rimmed baking sheet in the oven while it preheats.

2 Stud each orange with 10 whole cloves, and place on preheated baking sheet. Bake at 400°F for 1 hour or until soft. Remove pan from oven, and cool oranges slightly.

3 Quarter the oranges and place in the bottom of a stockpot. Pour in the port and wine, and bring mixture just to a simmer. Ladle into warmed mugs to serve.

3 NAVEL ORANGES

30 WHOLE CLOVES

1 (750-MILLILITER) BOTTLE PORT

1 (750-MILLILITER) BOTTLE LIGHT-BODIED RED WINE

The Origin of Happy Hour

AS YOU MIGHT EXPECT, the phrase "happy hour" was invented at sea. But it wasn't the blissful cocktails in sunset-soaked cabanas you're thinking of. In fact, the original happy hour had nothing to do with alcohol at all, and it looked a lot more like a boxing ring than a lazy afternoon.

In the 1920s, sailors in the U.S. Navy were restless. Days aboard the ship stretched dull and endless, especially on long voyages across the Atlantic and between port towns. For the sailors, docking on land meant dancing, meeting women, eating delicious local fare, and exploring cultures. At sea, they were stifled and homesick. To break up the monotony of the ocean, the Navy allotted sailors certain time periods for entertainment, which were soon dubbed "happy hours." Because they lived in cramped quarters below deck, sailors often preferred physical activity for their entertainment. Thus, the first happy hours were filled with wrestling and boxing matches—and the Navy sailors couldn't have been happier.

But happy hour soon took a less innocent turn: During Prohibition in the 1920s, the phrase became a slang term for secret booze-fueled gatherings. Friends would meet for "happy hour" before dinner, sneaking cocktails behind closed doors. Private speakeasies erupted; a different kind of entertainment was born. It would take many years for happy hour to move from intimate social circles to public watering holes.

In the 1970s and 1980s, happy hour began to resemble what we know it as today: a period of discounted food and drink prices, usually before the peak hours of the bar. Today's happy hour may have lost its Prohibition privacy—nearly every cabana has one—but it has certainly gained entertainment value, in respect to the Navy doldrums. To which we say: Bottoms up!

frozen margarita

(COCKTAIL ON LEFT)

3 CUPS (24 OUNCES) SUGAR

6 CUPS (48 OUNCES) WATER

1 CUP (8 OUNCES) SILVER TEQUILA

1 CUP (8 OUNCES) ORANGE LIQUEUR (SUCH AS TRIPLE SEC)

2 TABLESPOONS LIME ZEST

2 CUPS (16 OUNCES) FRESH LIME JUICE (ABOUT 16 LIMES)

GARNISH: LIME SLICES

No fiesta is complete without rounds of frozen margaritas. Try freezing margaritas in an electric ice-cream maker for extra slushiness.

SERVES 6 TO 8

1 Combine the sugar and water in a saucepan over medium-high. Cook, stirring constantly, 5 minutes or until sugar dissolves. Remove from heat, and cool completely; set aside.

2 Combine the tequila, liqueur, lime zest, lime juice, and reserved simple syrup.

3 Pour the mixture into a 4-quart container, and freeze 3 hours, stirring every 30 minutes to break up large ice crystals. Garnish, if desired.

frosty raspberry-lime margarita

(COCKTAIL ON RIGHT)

1½ CUPS (12 OUNCES) TEQUILA

1 CUP (8 OUNCES) ORANGE LIQUEUR (SUCH AS TRIPLE SEC)

4 CUPS FRESH OR FROZEN RASPBERRIES

½ CUP (4 OUNCES) FRESH LIME JUICE (ABOUT 4 LIMES)

⅔ CUP (ABOUT 4⅔ OUNCES) SUGAR

8 CUPS ICE

GARNISHES: FRESH RASPBERRIES, LIME WEDGES

Have a little fun with your traditional margarita recipe by adding fresh raspberry and lime flavors.

SERVES 8

Combine all the ingredients, in batches if necessary, in a blender, cover with lid, and process until smooth. Garnish, if desired.

watermelon-jalapeño margarita

For a spicy garnish, combine salt and chili powder on a shallow plate. Dip rims of glasses in lime juice or water, and twist in salt mixture to coat.

SERVES 6 TO 8

1 Process the watermelon, in batches, in a blender or food processor until smooth. Pour through a wire-mesh strainer, pressing with the back of a spoon; discard pulp and seeds.

2 Combine the watermelon liquid, tequila, and next 4 ingredients in a large pitcher. Cover and chill 1 hour (longer for a stronger pepper flavor). Serve over ice. Garnish, if desired.

8 CUPS SEEDED, CUBED WATERMELON

1½ CUPS (12 OUNCES) WHITE TEQUILA

½ CUP (4 OUNCES) ORANGE LIQUEUR (SUCH AS TRIPLE SEC)

½ CUP (4 OUNCES) FRESH LIME JUICE (ABOUT 4 LIMES)

¼ CUP (2 OUNCES) SIMPLE SYRUP (PAGE 17)

1 TO 2 JALAPEÑO CHILES, THINLY SLICED

GARNISHES: FRESH JALAPEÑO CHILE SLICES, WATERMELON WEDGES

watermelon daiquiri slush

9 CUPS SEEDED, CUBED WATERMELON

1 CUP (8 OUNCES) LIGHT RUM

¼ CUP (2 OUNCES) FRESH LIME JUICE

¼ CUP (2 OUNCES) SUGAR

1 (10-OUNCE) CAN FROZEN STRAWBERRY DAIQUIRI MIX, THAWED

Sweet watermelon and strawberries meet sharp lime juice in this cool, frosty sipper. Mix up a batch for your next pool party.

SERVES 8

1 Freeze half the watermelon.

2 Combine remaining watermelon and remaining ingredients in a blender, cover with lid, and process until smooth. Pour half of mixture into a pitcher. Add frozen melon to remaining mixture in blender, cover with lid, and process until smooth. Stir into pitcher.

tropical fruit slush

1 PINT PASSION FRUIT SORBET

1 CUP (8 OUNCES) GUAVA JUICE

1 CUP (8 OUNCES) PAPAYA JUICE

1 CUP (8 OUNCES) PASSION FRUIT-FLAVORED RUM

3 CUPS CRUSHED ICE

GARNISH: STAR FRUIT SLICES

Remember buying fruit slushies as a kid? Here's the adult version of those old summer must-haves—just as deliciously fruity, but now with a splash of rum.

SERVES 6

Combine the first 5 ingredients in a 7-cup blender (or in batches), cover with lid, and process until smooth. Garnish, if desired.

A beautiful and historic site, Cuba's Playa Daiquirí in Santiago de Cuba Province inspired Jennings Cox, the probable inventor of the iconic beverage, to name his drink after it.

seaside sunrise

Perfect for the beach, this blend of bright juices and passion fruit rum gets topped off with bubbly for a tropical twist on a mimosa.

SERVES 10

Combine the first 5 ingredients in a large pitcher. Pour into ice-filled glasses, and top off with sparkling wine, if desired. Garnish, if desired.

2 CUPS (16 OUNCES) FRESH PINEAPPLE JUICE

2 CUPS (16 OUNCES) ORANGE-MANGO JUICE

2 CUPS (16 OUNCES) PASSION FRUIT-FLAVORED RUM

1 CUP (8 OUNCES) CRANBERRY JUICE COCKTAIL

2 TABLESPOONS (1 OUNCE) GRENADINE (PAGE 23)

1 (750-MILLILITER) BOTTLE SPARKLING WINE (OPTIONAL)

GARNISHES: ORANGE SLICE AND LIME WEDGES

pineapple mojitos

(COCKTAIL SHOWN)

2 CUPS CUBED FRESH PINEAPPLE

16 FRESH MINT LEAVES

1 CUP LEMONGRASS SIMPLE
 SYRUP (PAGE 17)

1 CUP (8 OUNCES) FRESH LIME
 JUICE (ABOUT 8 LIMES)

1 CUP (8 OUNCES) WHITE RUM,
 CHILLED

1 (1-LITER) BOTTLE CLUB SODA,
 CHILLED

Refreshing Pineapple Mojitos get your party started in the right direction. An added plus is that the Lemongrass Simple Syrup can be prepared a day or so ahead.

SERVES 8

1 Muddle pineapple and mint in a pitcher.

2 Divide mixture among 8 stemless wineglasses or canning jars. Add 2 tablespoons each Lemongrass Simple Syrup, lime juice, and rum to each glass. Fill glasses three-fourths full with club soda. Stir in about ⅓ cup crushed ice. Serve immediately.

limoncello mojitos

½ CUP (4 OUNCES) FRESH LEMON
 JUICE (ABOUT 4 LEMONS)

⅓ CUP (ABOUT 2⅓ OUNCES)
 SUGAR

½ CUP FRESH MINT LEAVES

3 CUPS (24 OUNCES) LEMON
 LIQUEUR (SUCH AS
 LIMONCELLO), CHILLED

3 CUPS (24 OUNCES) CLUB SODA,
 CHILLED

GARNISHES: LEMON SLICES, FRESH
 MINT LEAVES

A citrusy new take on the classic cocktail, this mouthwatering concoction is perfect for the dog days of summer.

SERVES 6

1 Combine the first 3 ingredients in a pitcher. Crush with a muddler or wooden spoon until mint leaves are bruised and sugar has dissolved.

2 Fill pitcher with ice, and stir in limoncello and club soda.

pink bikini

(COCKTAIL SHOWN)

This is a sweet and refreshing cocktail that will easily become a favorite. As one online reviewer claims, "I have made this twice and since sharing it with neighbors, it has become a neighborhood hit. It's a drink that goes down pretty easy, so be careful to not have too many."

SERVES 10

Combine the first 3 ingredients in a large pitcher. Stir well, and serve over ice in rocks glasses. Garnish, if desired.

1 (1.75-LITER) BOTTLE RASPBERRY LEMONADE

1¾ CUPS (14 OUNCES) COCONUT RUM

1 CUP (8 OUNCES) AMARETTO

GARNISHES: FRESH RASPBERRIES, ORCHID BLOSSOMS

pink-a-colada

Cranberry juice lends a pinkish tint to this cocktail and contributes to its name—Pink-a-Colada. Brighten up this refreshing beverage with fresh pineapple and edible flowers.

SERVES 8

Combine the first 4 ingredients in a large pitcher. Stir well, and serve over ice in rocks glasses. Garnish, if desired.

3 CUPS (24 OUNCES) CRANBERRY JUICE COCKTAIL

2 CUPS (16 OUNCES) COCONUT WATER

1½ CUPS (12 OUNCES) FRESH PINEAPPLE JUICE

2 CUPS (16 OUNCES) COCONUT RUM

GARNISHES: PINEAPPLE WEDGES, TROPICAL FLOWERS

mango molada

Why should pineapples have all the fun? Mangoes shine in this fruity twist on the classic piña colada.

4 CUPS FRESH OR FROZEN MANGO CUBES

2 CUPS FRESH OR FROZEN PINEAPPLE CUBES

2 CUPS (16 OUNCES) MANGO RUM

1 CUP (8 OUNCES) COCONUT RUM

1 CUP (8 OUNCES) CREAM OF COCONUT

4 CUPS CRUSHED ICE

GARNISH: SUGARCANE SWIZZLE STICKS

SERVES 8

Combine the first 6 ingredients in a blender, in batches if necessary, cover with lid, and process until smooth. Garnish, if desired.

Bar Talk

FLAVORED RUM—

LESS POTENT THAN WHITE OR AGED RUM, FLAVOR-INFUSED RUM IS A TIKI BAR STANDARD FOR SIPPING OVER ICE OR MIXING IN FRUITY COCKTAILS.

Mango trees can grow to a height of 100 feet but most are pruned to make harvesting easier.

goombay smash

Nearly every drink menu in the Bahamas offers a Goombay Smash, though the drink varies from bar to bar. That's because Miss Emily, of Miss Emily's Blue Bee Bar, created the drink in the 1960s, and kept her recipe top secret. Legends say that Emily would prepare gallon-sized batches of the drink, so when customers would order it, they couldn't glimpse the recipe being made at the bar.

SERVES 8

1 Combine the brandy, coconut rum, 1¼ cups of the dark rum, and pineapple juice in a 1-gallon container.

2 Pour about 1½ cups pineapple juice mixture into ice-filled Collins glasses. Top off each serving with 2 tablespoons dark rum. Garnish, if desired.

⅔ CUP (ABOUT 6 OUNCES) APRICOT BRANDY

1¼ CUPS (10 OUNCES) COCONUT RUM

2¼ CUPS (18 OUNCES) DARK RUM

1 (46-OUNCE) CAN PINEAPPLE JUICE

GARNISHES: MARASCHINO CHERRIES, ORANGE WEDGES

Built in 1817, the lighthouse on Paradise Island is said to be the oldest working lighthouse in the Bahamas.

pacific punch

1 CUP (8 OUNCES) DARK RUM

1 CUP (8 OUNCES) LIGHT RUM

½ CUP (4 OUNCES) CRÈME DE BANANA

½ CUP (4 OUNCES) CRÈME DE CASSIS

¼ CUP (2 OUNCES) FRESH LIME JUICE

3 CUPS (24 OUNCES) FRESH PINEAPPLE JUICE

2 CUPS (16 OUNCES) CRANBERRY JUICE

GARNISHES: PINEAPPLE WEDGES, FRESH CRANBERRIES

Take a sip, close your eyes, and pretend you're lounging on an island somewhere in the Pacific. Or better yet, host a tropical party on your own turf, and serve this fruity punch to your island-dreaming friends.

SERVES 8

Combine the first 7 ingredients in a large pitcher. Serve over ice. Garnish, if desired.

Bar Talk

CRÈME LIQUEUR—
NOT TO BE CONFUSED WITH CREAM LIQUEUR, WHICH CONTAINS CREAM, THIS LIQUEUR IS FORTIFIED WITH SUGAR UNTIL IT REACHES THE CONSISTENCY OF SYRUP.

spiked lemonade

Start with lemon-flavored sparkling water or club soda, and add citrus-flavored vodka, lemon juice, sugar, and orange liqueur for an unforgettable summer lemonade cocktail. Buy extra ingredients—this one is guaranteed to be a party-pleaser.

SERVES 8

Combine the first 5 ingredients in a large pitcher. Serve over crushed ice. Garnish, if desired.

VARIATIONS:

spicy spiked honey lemonade: Substitute ¼ cup Jalapeño-Honey Syrup (page 18) for the sugar.

spiked pink lemonade: Add 2 tablespoons Grenadine (page 23) to the mix. Garnish with rapsberries or strawberries.

2   CUPS (16 OUNCES) LEMON-FLAVORED SPARKLING WATER OR CLUB SODA, CHILLED

½   CUP (4 OUNCES) CITRUS-FLAVORED VODKA, CHILLED

½   CUP (4 OUNCES) FRESH LEMON JUICE (ABOUT 4 LEMONS)

¼   CUP (2 OUNCES) SUGAR

¼   CUP (2 OUNCES) COINTREAU OR OTHER ORANGE LIQUEUR

GARNISH: LEMON SLICES

peach fuzzies

1 (12-OUNCE) CAN FROZEN PINK LEMONADE CONCENTRATE, SLIGHTLY THAWED

¾ CUP (6 OUNCES) VODKA

¾ CUP (6 OUNCES) WATER

4 CUPS PEELED AND CUBED FRESH, RIPE PEACHES (ABOUT 6 LARGE)

GARNISH: FRESH PEACH WEDGES

Serve these festive peach cocktails at an early afternoon barbecue. Frozen pink lemonade concentrate gives the drink its color and its sweet-tart flavor base. Add vodka, water, and ripe peaches for extra sweetness, and then process with crushed ice.

SERVES 10

Combine half quantities of the first 4 ingredients in a blender, cover with lid, and process until smooth, stopping to scrape down sides. Add ice to make 5 cups; process until smooth. Pour into a pitcher. Repeat procedure with remaining ingredients. Serve in hurricane glasses with a straw or a spoon. Garnish, if desired.

The aptly named Driftwood Beach off the Georgia coast is littered with sculptural tree branches due to erosion.

coastal skies

The name hints at the vivid blue color of this invigorating summer sipper that comes from the bright blue variety of curaçao.

SERVES 8

Combine the first 6 ingredients in an ice-filled pitcher. Garnish, if desired.

2   CUPS (16 OUNCES) PINEAPPLE-FLAVORED VODKA OR RUM

2   CUPS (16 OUNCES) BLUE CURAÇAO

1   CUP (8 OUNCES) AMARETTO

1   CUP (8 OUNCES) FRESH PINEAPPLE JUICE

1   CUP (8 OUNCES) FRESH LIME JUICE (ABOUT 8 LIMES)

1   CUP (8 OUNCES) SWEET-AND-SOUR MIX (PAGE 24) OR SIMPLE SYRUP (PAGE 17)

GARNISHES: LIME SLICES, PINEAPPLE WEDGES

Bar Talk

CURAÇAO—

A NATURALLY CLEAR, ORANGE LIQUEUR ORIGINALLY CREATED USING DRIED RINDS OF CURAÇAO'S NATIVE LARAHA CITRUS FRUIT AND DYED ELECTRIC BLUE OR ORANGE.

mint julep iced tea

8   FRESH MINT LEAVES

1   LEMON, SLICED

1   LIME, SLICED

1   CUP (8 OUNCES) BOURBON

3   CUPS (24 OUNCES) COLD
    SWEETENED TEA

GARNISHES: FRESH MINT SPRIGS,
    LEMON AND LIME SLICES

This tea holds all the tasty secrets of the mint julep—bracingly fragrant mint and the sweet burn of bourbon—along with fresh lemon, lime, and sweetened tea. Mix it up to create a summer-ready drink for the adults in your circle.

SERVES 6

Combine the first 3 ingredients in a 2-quart pitcher. Crush with a spoon until mint is bruised. Stir in bourbon and tea. Serve over ice. Garnish, if desired.

tropical champagne punch

(COCKTAIL FRONT LEFT, PAGE 224)

For the best flavor, chill all the ingredients before combining.

SERVES 12

Combine the first 5 ingredients in a large bowl. Stir in the sparkling wine. Serve over ice. Garnish, if desired.

- 2 CUPS (16 OUNCES) PINEAPPLE-MANGO JUICE
- 2 CUPS (16 OUNCES) FRESH ORANGE JUICE (ABOUT 8 ORANGES)
- 2 CUPS (16 OUNCES) CRANBERRY JUICE
- 2 CUPS (16 OUNCES) GUAVA NECTAR
- 1 CUP (8 OUNCES) APPLE JUICE
- 1 (750-MILLILITER) BOTTLE CHAMPAGNE

GARNISHES: SLICED STAR FRUIT, LIME WEDGES

mimosa

(COCKTAIL BACK RIGHT, PAGE 224)

This Sunday brunch staple gets an upgrade with a subtle hint of bitters and sugar cubes. Be sure to use freshly squeezed orange juice for a delicious sip.

SERVES 10

Combine the Champagne or prosecco and juice in a pitcher. Place a sugar cube in the bottom of each of 10 champagne flutes. Add a drop of bitters to each glass. Divide Champagne mixture evenly among prepared glasses. Garnish, if desired.

- 2 (750-MILLILITER) BOTTLES CHAMPAGNE OR PROSECCO
- 3½ CUPS FRESH ORANGE JUICE (ABOUT 14 ORANGES)
- 10 SUGAR CUBES
- 10 DROPS OF HOMEMADE PEACH-VANILLA BITTERS (PAGE 27)

GARNISH: ORANGE TWISTS

summer sangria

(COCKTAIL ON LEFT, PAGE 225)

Cool down on a warm afternoon with a batch—or two—of Summer Sangria.

SERVES 6

1 Combine all the ingredients in a large pitcher. Cover and chill at least 2 hours.

2 Add crushed ice to pitcher. Serve immediately.

1   (750-MILLILITER) BOTTLE VIOGNIER OR SAUVIGNON BLANC

½   CUP (4 OUNCES) PASSION FRUIT-, MANGO-, OR CITRUS-FLAVORED RUM OR VODKA

2   KIWIFRUIT, PEELED AND SLICED

1   MANGO, PEELED AND THINLY SLICED

1   CUP FRESH RASPBERRIES

¼   CUP SWEET-AND-SOUR MIX (PAGE 24) OR SIMPLE SYRUP (PAGE 17)

beaujolais it on me

(COCKTAIL ON RIGHT, PAGE 225)

Cointreau, orange juice, red wine, and club soda are the key ingredients to this special-occasion cocktail.

SERVES 8

1 Combine the first 3 ingredients in a large pitcher, stirring until sugar begins to dissolve. Quarter the grapefruit slices to make triangles; add to pitcher with orange slices, ginger slices, and wine. Cover and chill at least 8 hours or overnight.

2 Add the club soda to pitcher just before serving, and stir gently.

½   CUP (4 OUNCES) COINTREAU OR OTHER ORANGE LIQUEUR

½   CUP (4 OUNCES) FRESH ORANGE JUICE (ABOUT 2 ORANGES)

¼   CUP (2 OUNCES) SUGAR

1   SMALL GRAPEFRUIT, THINLY SLICED

1   ORANGE, THINLY SLICED

1   (1-INCH) PIECE FRESH GINGER, PEELED AND SLICED

1   (750-MILLILITER) BOTTLE LIGHT-BODIED RED WINE (SUCH AS BEAUJOLAIS)

2½ CUPS (20 OUNCES) CLUB SODA, CHILLED

MOCKTAILS

watermelon agua fresca

The types of aguas frescas available from street vendors in Mexico, Central America, and the Caribbean (shown in opposite photo) are as diverse as options for fruit. Watermelon is a popular favorite that has been described as "watermelon-scented water." The flavor doesn't overpower, but refreshes, especially on hot days.

SERVES 10

1 Process the watermelon in a blender until smooth.

2 Pour the mixture into a large bowl; stir in 8 cups water, sugar, and lime juice. Cover and chill at least 8 hours. Stir; serve in Collins glasses. Garnish, if desired.

VARIATION:

cucumber agua fresca: Substitute 6 cups peeled and cubed cucumber for the watermelon, and add ½ cup loosely packed fresh mint leaves.

6   CUPS SEEDED, CUBED WATERMELON

8   CUPS (64 OUNCES) WATER

½   CUP (4 OUNCES) SUGAR

½   CUP (4 OUNCES) FRESH LIME JUICE (ABOUT 4 LIMES)

GARNISH: WATERMELON WEDGES

Bar Talk

AGUA FRESCA—

TRANSLATED TO "FRESH WATER," AGUA FRESCA IS A REFRESHING BLENDED DRINK OF FRUIT, WATER, SUGAR, AND CITRUS THAT IS AN EQUALLY DELICIOUS COCKTAIL MIXER.

sailboat lemonade

Make sure to have this tart treat packed in a cooler for your next sailing adventure.

1¼ CUPS (10 OUNCES) SUGAR

½ CUP (4 OUNCES) BOILING WATER

1½ CUPS (12 OUNCES) FRESH LEMON JUICE (ABOUT 12 LEMONS)

4½ CUPS (36 OUNCES) COLD WATER

GARNISH: LEMON SLICES

SERVES 6

Combine the sugar and boiling water, stirring until sugar dissolves. Add the lemon juice and cold water; mix well. Chill and serve over ice. Garnish, if desired.

VARIATION:

pink sailboat lemonade (COCKTAIL SHOWN): Stir in ¾ cup (6 ounces) maraschino cherry juice. Garnish with maraschino cherries and lemon slices, if desired.

lemon-lime slush

Lemon and lime go together like peanut butter and jelly. In this kid-friendly slush, the sweet and citrusy flavors are kicked into overdrive. Be sure to have this on hand for the pool party.

1 (12-OUNCE) CAN FROZEN LEMONADE, THAWED

1 (12-OUNCE) CAN FROZEN LIMEADE, THAWED

6 CUPS CRUSHED ICE

5 CUPS (40 OUNCES) LEMON-LIME SODA (SUCH AS 7-UP), CHILLED

GARNISHES: LEMON SLICES, LIME SLICES

SERVES 8

1 Combine half of the lemonade, limeade, and ice in a blender, cover with lid, and process until smooth, stopping to scrape down sides. Pour the mixture into a 4-quart plastic container. Repeat procedure with remaining half. Freeze until firm.

2 Remove from freezer 30 minutes before serving; break into chunks. Add the soda; stir until slushy.

Based on the New Urbanism model, Seaside, Florida, provided the idyllic setting in the movie *The Truman Show.*

florida spritzer

Citrus and cinnamon combine in this spritzer for a crisp, spicy treat that rivals the Florida heat.

SERVES 4

1 Combine the first 3 ingredients in a saucepan. Bring to a boil over medium-high. Reduce heat, and simmer, uncovered, for 5 minutes. Discard cinnamon stick. Transfer mixture to a pitcher. Cover and chill 4 hours.

2 Pour ⅓ cup grapefruit mixture into each of 4 (8-ounce) ice-filled stemless champagne glasses or flutes. Top off with ginger ale; stir gently. Garnish, if desired.

1½ CUPS (12 OUNCES) FRESH RUBY
   RED GRAPEFRUIT JUICE

¼ CUP (2 OUNCES) SUGAR

1 (2-INCH) CINNAMON STICK

GINGER ALE

GARNISH: GRAPEFRUIT WEDGE

fruited mint tea

(COCKTAIL SHOWN)

In Jamaica, a traditional breakfast isn't complete without freshly cut fruit and black tea, served with optional cream and sugar. Here, the herbal and tropical tastes of Jamaica come out in an invigorating tea.

SERVES 6 TO 8

3 CUPS (24 OUNCES) BOILING WATER

4 REGULAR-SIZE TEA BAGS

12 FRESH MINT SPRIGS

1 CUP (8 OUNCES) SUGAR

¼ CUP (2 OUNCES) FRESH LEMON JUICE

1 CUP (8 OUNCES) FRESH ORANGE JUICE (ABOUT 4 ORANGES)

4 CUPS (32 OUNCES) WATER

GARNISHES: FRESH MINT SPRIGS, ORANGE WEDGES

1 Pour the boiling water over tea bags and mint sprigs; cover and let steep 5 minutes.

2 Remove the tea bags and mint, squeezing gently. Stir in the sugar and next 3 ingredients. Serve over ice. Garnish, if desired.

spiced cider tea

Enjoy sipping warm spiced cider around a crackling fire. Some versions are made with hard cider, but our recipe is family-friendly.

SERVES 6 TO 8

CHEESECLOTH

1 ORANGE

1 LEMON

2 CINNAMON STICKS

3 WHOLE CLOVES

4 CUPS (32 OUNCES) WATER

¼ CUP PACKED LIGHT BROWN SUGAR

4 FAMILY-SIZE TEA BAGS

3 CUPS (24 OUNCES) APPLE CIDER

GARNISH: CINNAMON STICKS

1 Cut several layers of cheesecloth into 8-inch squares. Cut 3 (1-inch) strips of peel each from orange and lemon; place in cheesecloth. Add the cinnamon sticks and cloves. Wrap and secure with string.

2 Bring 4 cups water to a boil in a saucepan. Add the spice packet and brown sugar, reduce heat, and simmer 10 minutes. Remove from heat, and add tea bags. Steep 5 minutes.

3 Remove the spice packet and tea bags. Stir in the cider. Juice the orange and lemon, and pour into cider mixture. Heat over medium until hot but not boiling. Serve in mugs.

Tea Trade

ACCORDING TO LEGEND, the first cup of tea was accidentally sipped about 5,000 years ago. The drinker, none other than the Emperor of China, woke to find tea leaves floating in his pot of boiling water one morning. He gamely took a sip of the liquid, curious about the dark color and fragrant smell emanating from the leaves. The taste was earthy and robust, and each sip had a meditative quality to it—the combination of hot water and pungent herbs opened his sinuses and calmed his nerves.

Soon tea became a staple of Chinese culture. Zen Buddhists revered the beverage, believing tea could strengthen spiritual connections. Monks began bringing tea with them on global missions, consuming it as part of their religious practices.

Tea circulated in Asia for centuries before it appeared in Western nations. As trade increased between Europe and Asia, talk of tea surfaced, and in 1560, the first shipment of tea arrived at elite Dutch parlors. The sacred leaves were rare and expensive at the time, and offering tea to visitors was a sign of great wealth. Demand for the exotic drink steadily increased across Europe, and by the end of the 17th century, England was the leading importer of tea. Tight ties with the East India Trading Company allowed most English citizens access to tea, and afternoon "tea time"—a healthier alternative to booze—became a daily ritual.

When European colonizers arrived in the Americas, they brought tea with them. Sugar plantations lent sugar to the table, and sweetened tea became wildly popular. "Tea punches," a mix of tea and spirits, were created in the 1830s. Then in 1904, at the St. Louis World's Fair, hot tea was poured over ice to make it more appealing in the hot summer weather—at long last, iced tea was born.

hibiscus tea punch

Accent the floral flavor of the hibiscus tea with sparkling apple cider. This cool drink fits perfectly at a family picnic or an afternoon poolside party with friends.

SERVES 6 TO 8

1 Pour the 4 cups boiling water over tea bags. Cover; steep 10 minutes. Discard the tea bags. Stir in the sugar until dissolved. Chill until ready to serve.

2 Stir in the sparkling cider, and serve over ice. Garnish, if desired.

4 CUPS (32 OUNCES) BOILING WATER

8 HIBISCUS OR RED ZINGER TEA BAGS

1½ CUPS (12 OUNCES) SUGAR

1 (25.4-OUNCE) BOTTLE SPARKLING APPLE CIDER, CHILLED

GARNISH: LEMON WEDGES

aloha punch

Whether you're hosting a luau party, a summer barbecue, or simply want a taste of the tropics, this fruity punch is for you.

SERVES 4 TO 6

Combine the first 5 ingredients in a large pitcher. Serve over crushed ice.

2 CUPS (16 OUNCES) FRESH PINEAPPLE JUICE

1 CUP (8 OUNCES) STRAWBERRY JUICE

1 CUP (8 OUNCES) GUAVA JUICE

1 CUP (8 OUNCES) PEAR NECTAR

1 CUP (8 OUNCES) ORANGE CARBONATED BEVERAGE (SUCH AS ORANGINA)

GARNISH: COCKTAIL UMBRELLAS

Bar Talk

HIBISCUS—

A TROPICAL PLANT IN THE MALLOW FAMILY, HIBISCUS FLOWER PETALS GIVE COLOR AND TARTNESS TO RED ZINGER TEA, COCKTAILS, AND SWEET AND SAVORY RECIPES.

mango smoothie

(COCKTAIL SHOWN)

2½ CUPS PEELED, PITTED, AND CHOPPED MANGO*

1 (6-OUNCE) CONTAINER VANILLA WHOLE MILK YOGURT

½ CUP (4 OUNCES) ORANGE-MANGO JUICE

1 CUP ICE CUBES

1 TABLESPOON HONEY

1 TABLESPOON (ABOUT ½ OUNCE) FRESH LIME JUICE

¼ TEASPOON GROUND CARDAMOM (OPTIONAL)

GARNISH: ORCHID BLOSSOM

Mango is a tropical fruit staple because of its incredible versatility in the kitchen. The sweet stone fruit can be used in salsas and marinades, on meat or mixed in salads, eaten raw or blended in smoothies. Mango's smooth flesh shines in this creamy drink.

SERVES 4

Combine the first 6 ingredients and cardamom, if desired, in a blender, cover with lid, and process until smooth. Garnish, if desired. Serve immediately.

*NOTE: Substitute 1 (16-ounce) package frozen chopped mango for the fresh mango, if desired.

berry refresher

2 CUPS HALVED FRESH STRAWBERRIES

1 (6-OUNCE) CAN UNSWEETENED ORANGE JUICE CONCENTRATE, THAWED

2 TABLESPOONS POWDERED SUGAR

1 (8-OUNCE) CONTAINER RASPBERRY YOGURT

10 ICE CUBES

For kids (and adults) who love snacking on strawberries and sugar, the Berry Refresher can't be beat. Fresh strawberries, frozen orange juice, and raspberry yogurt combine for a sweet-tart drink with a creamy finish.

SERVES 4

Combine all the ingredients in a blender, cover with lid, and process until smooth.

pineapple-apricot cooler

(COCKTAIL ON LEFT)

Classic piña colada flavors of pineapple and coconut mingle with sweet apricot nectar in this light and juicy cooler.

SERVES 4

Combine all the ingredients in a blender, cover with lid, and process until smooth.

2	CUPS ICE CUBES
1	(11-OUNCE) CAN APRICOT NECTAR, CHILLED
⅓	CUP SOUR CREAM OR PLAIN YOGURT
½	CUP (4 OUNCES) UNSWEETENED PINEAPPLE JUICE
3	TABLESPOONS SUGAR
¼	TEASPOON COCONUT EXTRACT
1	(8-OUNCE) CAN CRUSHED PINEAPPLE, UNDRAINED AND CHILLED

pom-berry shake

(COCKTAIL ON RIGHT)

Mixed berries and pomegranate-blueberry juice combine to create a "berry" tasty shake.

SERVES 4

Combine the first 4 ingredients in a blender, cover with lid, and process until smooth. Garnish, if desired.

½	CUP (4 OUNCES) POMEGRANATE-BLUEBERRY JUICE
1	(12-OUNCE) PACKAGE FROZEN MIXED BERRIES, SUCH AS STRAWBERRIES, RASPBERRIES, AND BLUEBERRIES
1	QUART VANILLA ICE CREAM
1	CUP (8 OUNCES) WHOLE MILK
	GARNISH: FRESH BERRIES

peachy dream

(COCKTAIL ON FRONT LEFT, PAGE 246)

Just what the name indicates—a peach lover's dream!

SERVES 4

Combine first 4 ingredients in a blender, cover with lid, and process until smooth. Garnish, if desired.

1   QUART VANILLA ICE CREAM

4   CUPS FRESH (OR 1 [16-OUNCE] PACKAGE FROZEN) SLICED PEACHES

½   TO 1 CUP (4 TO 8 OUNCES) FRESH ORANGE JUICE (ABOUT 2 TO 4 ORANGES)

⅛   TEASPOON ALMOND EXTRACT

GARNISHES: FRESH PEACH SLICES, GRANOLA

mint-chocolate chip shake

(COCKTAIL ON LEFT, PAGE 247)

A few drops of green food coloring lend just the right minty hue.

SERVES 4

Combine first 3 ingredients in a blender, cover with lid, and process until smooth. Add drops of food coloring to mixture, stirring to reach desired shade of green. Stir in the chocolate morsels. Pour into 4 parfait glasses. Garnish, if desired.

½   CUP (4 OUNCES) WHOLE MILK

1   QUART VANILLA ICE CREAM

¼   TEASPOON PEPPERMINT EXTRACT

GREEN FOOD COLORING

¼   CUP MINI CHOCOLATE MORSELS

GARNISH: FRESH MINT SPRIGS

butterscotch–sea salt shake

(COCKTAIL ON BACK RIGHT, PAGE 246)

Salty and sweet meet in delicious, decadent balance.

SERVES 3

1 Melt the butter and sugar in a saucepan over medium. Stir in the cream, and bring mixture just to a boil; remove from heat, and stir in the vanilla. Let cool completely; refrigerate until cold and thickened.

2 Combine the ice cream, milk, and ¾ cup caramel mixture in a blender, cover with lid, and process until smooth. Pour half of remaining caramel mixture into 3 glasses, coating sides. Top with ice-cream mixture. Drizzle evenly with remaining caramel mixture. Sprinkle with a pinch of sea salt.

4 OUNCES (½ CUP) BUTTER

¾ CUP FIRMLY PACKED LIGHT BROWN SUGAR

½ CUP (4 OUNCES) HEAVY WHIPPING CREAM

2 TEASPOONS (ABOUT ¼ OUNCE) VANILLA EXTRACT

1 QUART VANILLA ICE CREAM

¼ CUP (2 OUNCES) WHOLE MILK

COARSE SEA SALT

peanut butter–chocolate shake

(COCKTAIL ON RIGHT, PAGE 247)

We combine a favorite duo to create this Peanut Butter–Chocolate Shake—and top it off with peanut butter cup candy.

SERVES 4

1 Freeze 4 (8-ounce) glasses until very cold. Pour 2 tablespoons chocolate sauce in bottom half of each glass, coating sides. Keep chilled until ready to serve.

2 Combine milk, ice cream, and peanut butter in a blender, cover with lid, and process until smooth. Pour into prepared glasses. Garnish, if desired.

½ CUP (4 OUNCES) CHOCOLATE SAUCE OR CHOCOLATE SYRUP

1 CUP (8 OUNCES) WHOLE MILK

1 QUART VANILLA ICE CREAM

1 CUP CREAMY OR CHUNKY PEANUT BUTTER

GARNISH: CHOPPED PEANUT BUTTER CUP CANDY

triple chocolate slush

1 CUP (8 OUNCES) WHOLE MILK

⅓ CUP SUGAR

2 OUNCES SEMISWEET CHOCOLATE, CHOPPED

2 TABLESPOONS UNSWEETENED COCOA

1 CUP ICE CUBES

2 CUPS VANILLA ICE CREAM

CHOCOLATE SYRUP

GARNISHES: WHIPPED CREAM, SHAVED CHOCOLATE

Although there's a bit of ice cream in this recipe, the ice makes it lighter and less rich than a typical milk shake. To keep the syrup visible on the sides of the glass, put the glass in the freezer up to 30 minutes before adding the syrup.

SERVES 4

1 Combine the milk and sugar in a small saucepan over medium Cook, stirring often, 3 minutes or until sugar dissolves. Remove pan from heat, and add the chocolate and cocoa. Let stand 5 minutes; whisk until smooth. Let cool to room temperature, about 30 minutes.

2 Combine the ice cubes, milk mixture, and ice cream in a blender, cover with lid, and process until smooth and slushy. Pour the chocolate syrup down the insides of 4 glasses; pour in iced chocolate.

iced coffee frappé

(COCKTAIL SHOWN)

2 TABLESPOONS INSTANT ESPRESSO

½ CUP (4 OUNCES) DARK CHOCOLATE SYRUP

¼ CUP (2 OUNCES) SUGAR

1½ CUPS (12 OUNCES) BOILING WATER

2 CUPS (16 OUNCES) HALF-AND-HALF

1 QUART VANILLA ICE CREAM

2 CUPS (16 OUNCES) GINGER ALE

ADDITIONAL VANILLA ICE CREAM

This favorite is inspired by a recipe from the Junior League of Boca Raton.

SERVES 8 TO 10

1 Combine the first 4 ingredients in a large pitcher; let stand until cooled. Cover and chill at least 8 hours.

2 Combine the espresso mixture, half-and-half, and 1 quart ice cream in a punch bowl. Stir in the ginger ale. Ladle into glasses. Top with ice cream, if desired.

Bar
SNACKS

almond-stuffed dates

A sweet, satisfying bite that's both chewy and crunchy.

SERVES 4

1 Slowly feed the almonds through a food grinder fitted with a coarse plate. Switch to a fine grinding plate, and feed almonds through grinder 3 or 4 times until smooth. (Alternatively, process in a food processor until smooth.) Transfer to a bowl, and stir in the lemon zest.

2 Bring the water and sugar to a boil in a small saucepan. Reduce heat to medium-high. Add the butter and ground almonds, stirring vigorously until mixture leaves sides of pan. Transfer the mixture to a small bowl. Cover and let cool 5 minutes.

3 Cut a lengthwise slit down center of each date to (but not through) the bottom, leaving ends intact. Mold a heaping teaspoonful of almond paste into a football shape, and stuff inside date. Gently press sides until paste pushes up slightly above top of date. Pour the sugar onto a small plate. Roll each stuffed date in sugar. Garnish, if desired. Serve immediately.

1 CUP WHOLE BLANCHED TOASTED ALMONDS

1 TABLESPOON LEMON ZEST

2 TABLESPOONS WATER

6 TABLESPOONS SUGAR

1 TABLESPOON BUTTER

24 LARGE PITTED DATES

SUGAR

GARNISH: LEMON ZEST

marinated feta

Olive oil and a sprinkling of fresh herbs create an ultra-flavorful marinade for feta cheese. Serve on crackers or crusty bread.

SERVES 6

1 Combine the first 7 ingredients in a medium microwave-safe bowl. Microwave on HIGH for 1 minute. Let stand 10 minutes.

2 Cut the feta block into 16 (½-inch) cubes. Gently stir cheese into oil mixture. Cover and refrigerate 8 hours or overnight. Drain (reserve oil for a delicious homemade salad dressing) and serve.

1½ CUPS EXTRA-VIRGIN OLIVE OIL

2 TABLESPOONS CHOPPED FRESH OREGANO

2 TABLESPOONS CHOPPED FRESH THYME

2 TEASPOONS CHOPPED FRESH ROSEMARY

¼ TEASPOON BLACK PEPPERCORNS

3 GARLIC CLOVES, CHOPPED

2 FRESNO PEPPERS, SLICED

1 (8-OUNCE) BLOCK FETA CHEESE

buttery deviled eggs

8 LARGE EGGS

2 TEASPOONS CHAMPAGNE VINEGAR

1 TEASPOON EXTRA-VIRGIN OLIVE OIL

½ TEASPOON KOSHER SALT

¼ TEASPOON FRESHLY GROUND BLACK PEPPER

2 MEDIUM RADISHES, FINELY DICED (ABOUT ⅓ CUP)

1½ OUNCES (3 TABLESPOONS) UNSALTED BUTTER, SOFTENED

¼ CUP MAYONNAISE

2 TEASPOONS DIJON MUSTARD

¼ CUP MICROGREENS

With roots in ancient Rome, deviled eggs first appear in a 13th-century Andalusian cookbook. Choose arugula, basil, or mustard microgreens for a peppery and pretty finish.

SERVES 8

1 Arrange the eggs in a single layer in a large saucepan with enough salted water to cover. Bring to a boil; cook 1 minute. Cover pan; remove from heat. Let stand 8 minutes; drain.

2 Place the eggs under cold running water until just cool enough to handle. Tap the eggs on a hard surface until cracks form; peel. Discard shells.

3 Combine the vinegar, oil, ¼ teaspoon of the salt, ⅛ teaspoon of the pepper, and radishes in a small bowl; toss to coat. Set aside.

4 Slice the eggs in half lengthwise; carefully remove yolks. Place the egg yolks, butter, mayonnaise, and mustard in the bowl of a food processor; process until smooth and fluffy, scraping down sides as necessary. Stir in remaining ¼ teaspoon salt and remaining ⅛ teaspoon pepper.

5 Spoon or pipe the yolk mixture evenly into egg white halves (about 1 tablespoon per egg half). Top the filled eggs evenly with radish mixture. Arrange egg halves on a serving plate, and sprinkle evenly with microgreens.

Happy hour starts as early as 3 in the afternoon at tapas bars like El Picoteo at Hotel El Convento in Old San Juan, Puerto Rico.

marinated peppers, artichokes, and olives

Roasting the peppers adds a subtle, smoky flavor to this super-easy and flavorful appetizer. Serve in small bowls as an antipasto along with breadsticks, aged cheese, and cured meats.

SERVES 8

1 Preheat the broiler. Cut the bell peppers in half lengthwise; discard seeds and membranes. Place the pepper halves, skin sides up, on an aluminum foil-lined baking sheet. Broil 6 inches from heat, turning once, 15 minutes or until blackened and charred. Place the peppers in a large zip-top plastic bag, and seal. Let stand 15 minutes. Peel and discard skins; cut peppers into strips.

2 Combine the peppers and remaining ingredients in a large bowl. Transfer to 2 (1-quart) jars, if desired. Store in the refrigerator up to 3 weeks.

6   RED BELL PEPPERS
2   (14-OUNCE) CANS ARTICHOKE BOTTOMS, DRAINED AND QUARTERED
5   GARLIC CLOVES, SLICED
1   CUP MIXED OLIVES
¾   CUP EXTRA-VIRGIN OR VIRGIN OLIVE OIL
⅓   CUP SHERRY VINEGAR
1   TEASPOON DRIED ITALIAN SEASONING
½   TEASPOON SALT
½   TEASPOON COARSELY GROUND BLACK PEPPER

grilled padrón peppers

If these local favorites are not at your market, look for peppers labeled "shishitos," or for guaranteed heat, try jalapeños instead.

SERVES 8

1 Preheat the grill to medium (350° to 450°F). Brush the peppers with olive oil, and sprinkle with sea salt.

2 Grill, turning occasionally, 5 to 7 minutes or until skin slightly blisters. Sprinkle with additional sea salt, if desired.

1   POUND PADRÓN PEPPERS
2   TABLESPOONS OLIVE OIL
SEA SALT

avocado salsa verde

Made with fresh tomatillos, jalapeño chile, cilantro, and avocado, this will be a hands-down favorite with partygoers.

SERVES 4

- 1 TO 1¼ POUNDS TOMATILLOS (ABOUT 10)
- ¼ SWEET ONION, CHOPPED
- 2 GARLIC CLOVES
- 1 JALAPEÑO CHILE, SEEDED AND CHOPPED
- ½ CUP LOOSELY PACKED FRESH CILANTRO
- 2 TABLESPOONS FRESH LIME JUICE
- 1 RIPE AVOCADO, PITTED AND CHOPPED
- 1½ TEASPOONS KOSHER SALT

1 Peel the husks from the tomatillos, and rinse under cold water until they are no longer sticky. Cut into chunks, and place in a food processor.

2 Add the onion, garlic, and pepper, and process until mixture is very finely chopped. Add the cilantro and lime juice, and process until finely chopped. Add the avocado and salt, and pulse until blended.

smoky orange-jicama salsa

Oranges and chipotle peppers create a delightful sweet-smoky combo that is tasty on many types of meat, from mild seafood to hearty steaks. Jicama is a turnip-shaped root vegetable with a very mild taste and a pleasant crunch.

SERVES 4

- 4 NAVEL ORANGES, PEELED AND CUT INTO SEGMENTS
- 1 CUP CHOPPED JICAMA
- ½ CUP CHOPPED RED BELL PEPPER
- ¼ CUP THINLY SLICED RED ONION
- 1 TEASPOON ORANGE ZEST
- ½ TEASPOON GROUND CUMIN
- ¼ CUP FRESH ORANGE JUICE (ABOUT 1 ORANGE)
- 1 CHOPPED CANNED CHIPOTLE PEPPER IN ADOBO SAUCE
- ½ TEASPOON SALT

1 Combine the first 6 ingredients in a bowl, breaking orange segments into pieces if large.

2 Combine the orange juice, chipotle pepper, and salt; stir into orange mixture. Cover and chill until ready to serve.

mango-lime salsa

The sweet flavor of mango meets its spicy match with jalapeño chiles, scallion, and cilantro in this salsa.

SERVES 4

Grate the zest from the limes to measure ½ teaspoon; place zest in a bowl. Peel and section the limes. Coarsely chop segments, and add to zest. Stir in the mangoes and remaining ingredients. Set aside until ready to serve.

2   LIMES

2   LARGE MANGOES, PEELED AND DICED

1   SCALLION, THINLY SLICED

¼   CUP DICED RED BELL PEPPER

2   TABLESPOONS CHOPPED FRESH CILANTRO

1   JALAPEÑO CHILE, SEEDED AND MINCED

¼   TEASPOON SALT

salsa fresca

(SALSA SHOWN PAGE 260)

A food processor gives this salsa a fine texture.

SERVES 4 TO 6

Combine all the ingredients in a food processor, cover, and pulse until evenly chopped. Cover and chill until ready to serve.

9   LARGE PLUM TOMATOES (ABOUT 4 POUNDS), SEEDED AND COARSELY CHOPPED

½   SMALL ONION, CUT INTO PIECES

2   GARLIC CLOVES, CHOPPED

1   TO 2 SERRANO CHILES, SEEDED AND CHOPPED

1   CUP LOOSELY PACKED FRESH CILANTRO LEAVES AND STEMS

1   TEASPOON SALT

1   TEASPOON LIME ZEST

2   TABLESPOONS FRESH LIME JUICE

Thousands of small islands make up the Greek Isles, but just 227 of them are inhabited.

taramasalata

Taramasalata is a creamy Greek dip comprised of milk-soaked bread and fish roe. Reserve black roe for other uses; it will turn this dip an unappetizing gray color.

SERVES 4

1 Tear the bread into pieces, and place in a small bowl. Drizzle milk over bread, tossing to moisten.

2 Combine soaked bread, tarama, and next 5 ingredients in a food processor, cover with lid, and process until smooth. With processor running, slowly add the olive oil through food chute, processing until mixture is mousse-like and fluffy. If too thick, add 2 tablespoons water to thin slightly.

3 Spoon into a bowl; cover and chill at least 1 hour. Top with additional tarama and chopped fresh chives. Serve with the pita chips.

3 (1-OUNCE) SLICES WHITE BREAD, CRUSTS REMOVED

¼ CUP (2 OUNCES) WHOLE MILK

¼ CUP TARAMA, CARP ROE, OR CAVIAR, PLUS MORE FOR GARNISH

2 TABLESPOONS FRESH LEMON JUICE

4 TEASPOONS CHOPPED SHALLOT

¾ TEASPOON MINCED GARLIC

⅛ TEASPOON SWEET OR SMOKED SWEET PAPRIKA

⅛ TEASPOON FRESHLY GROUND BLACK PEPPER

½ CUP OLIVE OIL

CHOPPED FRESH CHIVES

PITA CHIPS

smoky, buttery crab claws

Sweet, buttery crab flesh meets smoky bacon in this irresistibly savory dish.

SERVES 8

2   LEAN SMOKED BACON SLICES, CHOPPED

4   OUNCES (½ CUP) BUTTER

3   GARLIC CLOVES, MINCED

2   SCALLIONS, THINLY SLICED

2   TABLESPOONS FRESH LEMON JUICE

1   TABLESPOON WORCESTERSHIRE SAUCE

1   POUND CRAB CLAWS

2   TEASPOONS CHOPPED FRESH FLAT-LEAF PARSLEY

FRENCH BREAD

1 Cook the bacon in a skillet over medium-high heat until crisp. Remove with a slotted spoon to paper towels to drain, and discard drippings. Crumble.

2 Melt the butter in skillet; stir in garlic and scallions. Cook, stirring often, 2 minutes.

3 Stir in the lemon juice, Worcestershire, and crab claws; cook 2 to 3 minutes or until hot. Stir in the parsley and bacon. Serve immediately with the French bread.

Maine's Portland Head Light on Cape Elizabeth was first lit in 1791 with whale oil lamps.

maine crab cakes
with lime mayo

Top mini crab cakes with homemade lime mayo and sliced chives for an eye-catching and delicious appetizer.

SERVES 4

1 Pick crabmeat, removing any bits of shell. Combine the crabmeat, ¼ cup of the panko, and next 10 ingredients in a large bowl; mix with hands until fully incorporated.

2 Shape the mixture into 8 patties (about 2 tablespoons each). Carefully dredge patties in remaining ½ cup panko.

3 Heat the oil in a large nonstick skillet over medium-high until hot. Add the crab cakes; cook 2 minutes on each side or until golden. Top with the Lime Mayo and chives.

lime mayo

Combine 1 tablespoon finely grated lime zest, 1 tablespoon fresh lime juice, and 1 cup mayonnaise. Finely grate 1 peeled garlic clove with a fine Microplane grater or finely mince with a chef's knife. Stir the garlic into mayonnaise. MAKES 1 CUP

½ POUND FRESH LUMP CRABMEAT, DRAINED

¾ CUP PANKO (JAPANESE BREADCRUMBS) OR 2 TABLESPOONS FINE, DRIED BREADCRUMBS

2 TABLESPOONS SLICED SCALLION

1 TABLESPOON FINELY CHOPPED FRESH FLAT-LEAF PARSLEY

1½ TEASPOONS FINELY CHOPPED FRESH TARRAGON

1½ TEASPOONS FINELY CHOPPED FRESH CILANTRO

¼ TEASPOON SMOKED PAPRIKA

⅛ TO ¼ TEASPOON CAYENNE PEPPER

⅛ TEASPOON KOSHER SALT

1 LARGE EGG WHITE, LIGHTLY BEATEN

3 TABLESPOONS HEAVY CREAM

2 TABLESPOONS MAYONNAISE

1 TABLESPOON CANOLA OIL

LIME MAYO

CHOPPED FRESH CHIVES

Tiki Food Culture

ERNEST GANTT AND HIS WIFE, SUNNY SUND, launched a tidal wave of a trend when they brought island kitsch and exotic South Seas flavors to America in the 1950s at their Don the Beachcomber restaurant in California. From flaming torches and grass skirts to lush floral leis and mai tais garnished with paper umbrellas, their alluring Polynesian-themed atmosphere provided an escape where patrons could get lost for a while.

This was no place to find mid-century mainstream fare like meatloaf, lima beans, and mashed potatoes. Here, diners could immerse themselves in a faux far-flung fantasy from the moment they crossed the threshold. Exotic surrounds demanded an exotic menu and the Beachcomber served it up. Patrons loved it all. Rumaki (chicken livers and water chestnuts wrapped in a crisp bacon cloak) suddenly was all the rage. Crab Rangoon and tender pork-filled potstickers with soy dipping sauce became the new delicacies of cocktail hour. Flaming pu pu platters (skewered raw beef cooked at the table) were a novel part of many Beachcomber meals, and countless restaurants copied the experience.

Tiki culture expanded our horizons and palates at a time when ethnic food was often relegated to an off-the-beaten path borough or corner of town. This was an all-new cuisine inspired by uncommon flavors, and it primed palates for more. Whether it's Spanish-style tapas or Greek *Taramasalata* (page 265), our love affair with faraway flavors continues.

ceviche verde

¾ CUP FRESH LIME JUICE (ABOUT
6 LIMES)

¼ CUP FRESH LEMON JUICE
(ABOUT 2 LEMONS)

¼ CUP FINELY DICED WHITE
ONION

1 POUND SKINLESS HALIBUT
FILLETS, CUT INTO SMALL
PIECES

¾ CUP FINELY CHOPPED JICAMA

⅓ CUP CHOPPED FRESH CILANTRO

2 TABLESPOONS EXTRA-VIRGIN
OLIVE OIL

¾ TEASPOON SALT

¼ TEASPOON GROUND CUMIN

3 MEDIUM TOMATILLOS, HUSKED
AND DICED

2 SERRANO CHILES, SEEDED AND
MINCED

1 RIPE AVOCADO, PITTED AND
DICED

TORTILLA CHIPS OR TOSTADAS

Spicy chiles, cumin, jicama, cilantro and fresh citrus juice intensify the sweet flavors of halibut in this mouthwatering appetizer. Scoop with tortilla chips, if desired, or spread on tostadas for a light dinner.

SERVES 10

1 Combine the first 4 ingredients in a large glass or ceramic bowl, gently pressing down to cover fish with liquid. Cover and refrigerate 3 hours or until fish is opaque in center, stirring occasionally. Drain, reserving ⅓ cup liquid.

2 Combine the jicama and next 7 ingredients in a large glass or ceramic bowl. Stir in the fish mixture and reserved liquid. Cover and refrigerate 1 hour. Serve with chips or tostadas.

coconut unfried shrimp

These delectable shrimp are dipped in egg whites (instead of whole eggs), breaded, and then baked rather than deep-fried.

SERVES 4

1 Preheat the oven to 375°F. Combine the first 3 ingredients and ¼ teaspoon of the cayenne pepper in a small bowl. Set aside until ready to serve.

2 Combine remaining ¼ teaspoon cayenne pepper, flour, and salt in a large zip-top plastic bag. Whisk together the egg whites and 2 tablespoons water in a shallow dish. Combine the panko, coconut, and oil in a separate shallow dish.

3 Place the shrimp in bag with flour mixture, and shake to coat well. Dip the shrimp in egg white mixture, and roll in coconut mixture.

4 Place a wire rack inside a large baking pan. Coat baking rack with cooking spray. Arrange the shrimp in a single layer on rack, and bake at 375°F for 5 to 7 minutes or until golden brown and cooked through. Serve with reserved sauce.

¼ CUP ORANGE MARMALADE

1   TABLESPOON FRESH LEMON JUICE

2   TEASPOONS WHOLE-GRAIN MUSTARD

½   TEASPOON CAYENNE PEPPER

¼   CUP (ABOUT 1 OUNCE) ALL-PURPOSE FLOUR

½   TEASPOON SALT

2   LARGE EGG WHITES

2   TABLESPOONS WATER

¾   CUP PANKO (JAPANESE BREADCRUMBS)

½   CUP SWEETENED FLAKED COCONUT

2   TABLESPOONS CANOLA OIL

1½ POUNDS LARGE RAW SHRIMP (ABOUT 24), PEELED AND DEVEINED

glazed honey-garlic chicken wings

For a tasty alternative to classic Buffalo wings, serve these sweet and tangy grilled wings.

SERVES 4 TO 6

4 GARLIC CLOVES, MINCED

1 TABLESPOON GRATED FRESH GINGER

1 TABLESPOON MINCED FRESH CILANTRO

1 TABLESPOON LOWER-SODIUM SOY SAUCE

1 TABLESPOON FISH SAUCE

1 TABLESPOON HONEY

1 TEASPOON ASIAN CHILI-GARLIC SAUCE

½ TEASPOON CURRY POWDER

1 POUND CHICKEN DRUMETTES

1 Combine the first 8 ingredients in a small bowl, stirring with a whisk. Place the chicken in a large zip-top plastic bag. Pour the the marinade over chicken, seal bag, and toss gently to coat. Refrigerate at least 6 hours or overnight.

2 Preheat the grill to medium (350° to 450°F). Drain and discard marinade. Grill the chicken, turning occasionally, 35 minutes or until golden brown on all sides.

beef tenderloin yakitori

A Japanese street food that's as pretty as it is simple to make.

SERVES 6 TO 8

1 Soak the skewers in water at least 30 minutes. Combine 1 tablespoon each of the soy sauce, mirin, and sake in a medium bowl. Add the beef, tossing to coat. Let stand 30 to 90 minutes.

2 Combine remaining 3 tablespoons each soy sauce and mirin, remaining 1 tablespoon sake, and sugar in a small saucepan over medium-high. Simmer 5 to 8 minutes or until glaze is slightly syrupy. Set aside.

3 Combine the scallions and sesame oil; toss well. Thread scallion pieces and beef alternately onto skewers. Cover and chill until ready to grill.

4 Preheat grill to medium (350° to 450°F). Grill skewers 1 minute. Turn skewers over; brush with glaze, and grill 1 to 2 minutes or desired degree of doneness. Garnish, if desired.

24 (6-INCH) BAMBOO SKEWERS

¼ CUP LOWER-SODIUM SOY SAUCE

¼ CUP MIRIN

2 TABLESPOONS SAKE

1 POUND BEEF TENDERLOIN, CUT INTO 1-INCH CUBES

2 TABLESPOONS SUGAR

1 BUNCH SCALLIONS, CUT INTO 1-INCH PIECES

1 TEASPOON SESAME OIL

GARNISH: SESAME SEEDS

Metric Equivalents

The recipes that appear in this cookbook use the standard United States method for measuring liquid and dry or solid ingredients (teaspoons, tablespoons, and cups). The information in the following charts is provided to help cooks outside the U.S. successfully use these recipes. All equivalents are approximate.

Metric Equivalents for Different Types of Ingredients

A standard cup measure of a dry or solid ingredient will vary in weight depending on the type of ingredient. A standard cup of liquid is the same volume for any type of liquid. Use the following chart when converting standard cup measures to grams (weight) or milliliters (volume).

Standard Cup	Fine Powder (ex. flour)	Grain (ex. rice)	Granular (ex. sugar)	Liquid Solids (ex. butter)	Liquid (ex. milk)
1	140 g	150 g	190 g	200 g	240 ml
¾	105 g	113 g	143 g	150 g	180 ml
⅔	93 g	100 g	125 g	133 g	160 ml
½	70 g	75 g	95 g	100 g	120 ml
⅓	47 g	50 g	63 g	67 g	80 ml
¼	35 g	38 g	48 g	50 g	60 ml
⅛	18 g	19 g	24 g	25 g	30 ml

Useful Equivalents for Liquid Ingredients by Volume

¼ tsp					=	1 ml	
½ tsp					=	2 ml	
1 tsp					=	5 ml	
3 tsp	=	1 Tbsp		=	½ fl oz	=	15 ml	
		2 Tbsp	=	⅛ cup	=	1 fl oz	=	30 ml
		4 Tbsp	=	¼ cup	=	2 fl oz	=	60 ml
		5 ⅓ Tbsp	=	⅓ cup	=	3 fl oz	=	80 ml
		8 Tbsp	=	½ cup	=	4 fl oz	=	120 ml
		10 ⅔ Tbsp	=	⅔ cup	=	5 fl oz	=	160 ml
		12 Tbsp	=	¾ cup	=	6 fl oz	=	180 ml
		16 Tbsp	=	1 cup	=	8 fl oz	=	240 ml
		1 pt	=	2 cups	=	16 fl oz	=	480 ml
		1 qt	=	4 cups	=	32 fl oz	=	960 ml
						33 fl oz	=	1000 ml	= 1 l

Useful Equivalents for Dry Ingredients by Weight

(To convert ounces to grams, multiply the number of ounces by 30.)

1 oz	=	¹⁄₁₆ lb	=	30 g
4 oz	=	¼ lb	=	120 g
8 oz	=	½ lb	=	240 g
12 oz	=	¾ lb	=	360 g
16 oz	=	1 lb	=	480 g

Useful Equivalents for Length

(To convert inches to centimeters, multiply the number of inches by 2.5.)

1 in			=	2.5 cm		
6 in	=	½ ft	=	15 cm		
12 in	=	1 ft	=	30 cm		
36 in	=	3 ft	=	1 yd	=	90 cm	
40 in			=	100 cm	=	1 m

Useful Equivalents for Cooking/Oven Temperatures

	Fahrenheit	Celsius	Gas Mark
Freeze Water	32° F	0° C	
Room Temperature	68° F	20° C	
Boil Water	212° F	100° C	
Bake	325° F	160° C	3
	350° F	180° C	4
	375° F	190° C	5
	400° F	200° C	6
	F	220° C	7
	425° F	230° C	8
Broil	450° F		Grill

INDEX

Which Coastal Cocktail Are You?

WHAT'S YOUR FAVORITE TIME OF DAY TO IMBIBE?
- A. Happy hour
- B. Nighttime
- C. At brunch
- D. Depends what time the party is!
- E. On a sunny afternoon in the sand

WHO'S YOUR FANTASY CELEBRITY BARTENDER?
- A. Daniel Craig
- B. George Clooney
- C. Harry Connick, Jr.
- D. Rihanna
- E. Jimmy Buffett

YOUR FRIENDS WOULD DESCRIBE YOU AS. . .
- A. Stylish
- B. Sophisticated
- C. Reliable
- D. A social butterfly
- E. Easygoing

WHAT'S YOUR DREAM JOB?
- A. Celebrity stylist
- B. Architect
- C. Best-selling author
- D. Event planner
- E. Beach bum

IT'S SATURDAY AFTERNOON. WHAT'S YOUR DRESS CODE?
- A. A cute swimsuit with a chic sarong
- B. A designer tunic with white linen pants
- C. Shorts and a tank with a cute straw hat
- D. A bright sundress and flip flops
- E. Denim shorts and a bikini top

WHAT'S ON YOUR BEACH PLAYLIST?
- A. Beyoncé
- B. Vintage jazz
- C. A carefully curated Spotify playlist
- D. The Beach Boys
- E. Bob Marley

YOU'RE AT A BEACH PARTY. WHAT ARE YOU DOING?
- A. Chatting with everyone
- B. At a cocktail table by the pool
- C. Tidying up the party space
- D. Making sure all the cups are filled
- E. Jamming to an acoustic guitar around a bonfire

WHAT'S YOUR DREAM BEACH VACATION?
- A. Grand Cayman with your closest girlfriends
- B. Poolside service in St. Barths
- C. A culinary adventure on the Amalfi Coast
- D. Renting a big house in the Outer Banks with extended family
- E. Hitting all the local music joints in Key West

WHAT'S YOUR SPIRIT SEA CREATURE?
- A. Mermaid
- B. Starfish
- C. Sea turtle
- D. Dolphin
- E. Plankton

IF YOU WON THE LOTTERY, WHAT WOULD YOU DO WITH THE MONEY?
- A. Spend three months eating and shopping in the Mediterranean
- B. Give half to charity and then have a party to celebrate
- C. Fix up the house and invest the rest
- D. Take your closest family and friends on an extravagant vacation
- E. Buy a house in Costa Rica and learn to surf

Mostly As
Pink Bikini (page 209)
Just like the suit this drink is named for, you're sassy, sweet, and timeless. The Pink Bikini is the perfect combination of fun, great taste, and presentation.

Mostly Bs
Basil Tonic (page 113)
First impressions are key, and you're always giving off a good one, just like this beloved, refreshing drink. Simple, yet effortlessly sophisticated, this cocktail is the perfect twist on the traditional.

Mostly Cs
Seaside Sunrise (page 205)
"Early to bed, early to rise" may be your motto (apropos for this tasty brunch beverage) but you also love a good time. The Seaside Sunrise is a bright and bubbly combination of citrus and tropical juices topped off with sparkling wine.

Mostly Ds
Pineapple Mojitos (page 206)
You never make just one cocktail—because you always have a posse with you! Our big batch recipe for Pineapple Mojitos satisfies cocktail cravings and a crowd.

Mostly Es
The Coastal Margarita (page 44)
There's only one word to describe you (and your margaritas): Chill. Your beach to-do list is usually blank, and you prefer it that way. With your easygoing attitude, you're typically up for anything—as long as there's a live band, a view, and a round of drinks involved.